Mingled Voices 3
International Proverse Poetry Prize Anthology 2018
Proverse Hong Kong
2019

Supported by

Hong Kong Arts Development Council fully supports freedom of artistic expression. The views and opinions expressed in this project do not represent the stand of the Council.

MINGLED VOICES 3 is an anthology of one hundred and thirty-nine poems, the work of eighty-nine poets, selected from those which were entered in the third annual international competition for the International Proverse Poetry Prize in May - July 2018.

The International Proverse Poetry Prize was jointly founded in 2016 by Dr Gillian Bickley and Dr Verner Bickley MBE, in association with the annual international Proverse Prize for unpublished book-length fiction, non-fiction or poetry, submitted in English, which they also founded, in 2008.

Poems could be submitted on any subject or topic, chosen by each poet, or on the subject chosen for 2018 by the Administrators, "Refuge". There was a free choice of form and style.

Included in the anthology are the poems that won the first, second, and third prizes. Selection to appear in the anthology was also awarded as a prize by the judges for the Prize.

Poems were submitted from Australia, Austria, Belgium, Canada, the Czech Republic, France, Greece, Hong Kong, India, Indonesia, Italy, Macau, Malaysia, New Zealand, Singapore, Sweden, Turkey, the Peoples' Republic of China, the United Kingdom, the United Arab Emirates and the United States of America.

The countries of birth of these poets include Canada, Cuba, Germany, Hong Kong, Italy, the Netherlands, Poland, Spain, the United Kingdom, the United States of America, and Wales.

Some are new or young writers. Others are already well-published as poets, whether in magazines and journals or in book form; some with several published poetry collections of their own. Some are prize-winning writers and writers who have participated in poetry festivals and other prestigious events.

Mingled Voices 3
International Proverse Poetry Prize Anthology
2018

Contributors

Abigail Taylor, Akin Jeje, Allegra Jostad Silberstein,
Andrew Sutherland, Angelo Rizzi, Anson Wang, Anthea Yip,
Antony Huen, Arthur Allen, Aya Mohtadi, Belle Ling,
Benny Chia, Birgit Bunzel Linder, Bruce Dodson,
Bruce Arlen Wasserman, Carol Flake Chapman, Carol Krauss,
Christos Koukis, Cindy Wyles, D. J. Hamilton, Danny Poon,
David Vognar, Edward Tiesse, Elbert Lee, Elizabeth Grobler,
Elizabeth (Libby) Wong, Franz Krabel, George Watt,
Giovena Wang Songwenjia, Halil Suat Saraç,
Hasan Erkek, Hayley Ann Solomon, Helen Davis,
Hilary Faulkner, Ho Cheung Lee, Indran Amirthanayagam,
J. P. Linstroth, Jack Mayer, Jade Hui, Jeddie Sophronius,
Jemima Law, Joanna Radwańska-Williams,
John Dorrell, Jonathan Hart,
Josie Chambers, José Manuel Sevilla, Joy Al-Sofi, Jun Pan,
Kate Hawkins, Keith Nunes, Laura Solomon,
Lauriane Chappé, Lonnie Monka, Luisa Ternau,
Lynda Lambert, Maria Elena Blanco, Matthew Harris,
Meghan Kelsey, Melissa Reed, Michael Gould, N. Noéll,
Neil Douglas, Olga Walló, Paola Caronni, Patience O'Neill,
Patrick Reardon, Pei Kai Cheng, Peter Verbica, Rachel Leung,
Richard Westley, Rochelle Potkar, Roger Uren, Rony Nair,
Sally Younger, Sanja Särman, Selena Liang, Simona Rackova,
Solomon Au Yeung, Stephen Herman, Steve Borst,
Steven Harz, Sui Ping Au Yeung, Susan Phillips,
Susan Lavender, Thea Biesheuvel, Ty Newcomb,
Vinita Agrawal, Vinni Relwani, Zachary Knox.

Editors
Gillian Bickley · Verner Bickley

Proverse Hong Kong

Mingled Voices 3
International Proverse Poetry Prize Anthology 2018
edited by Gillian Bickley and Verner Bickley.
Alternate Edition (POD): 978-988-8491-56-8
Published in Hong Kong by Proverse Hong Kong, April 2019
1st published in paperback in Hong Kong by Proverse Hong Kong,
April 2019.
ISBN: 978-988-8491-55-1
Copyright © Proverse Hong Kong 2019.
Each author retains the copyright in the poem(s)
that appear with his/her own name.

Distribution (Hong Kong and worldwide):
The Chinese University Press of Hong Kong,
The Chinese University of Hong Kong,
Shatin, New Territories, Hong Kong SAR.
E-mail: cup-bus@cuhk.edu.hk; Web: www.chineseupress.com

Distribution and other enquiries to:
Proverse Hong Kong, P.O. Box 259, Tung Chung Post Office,
Tung Chung, Lantau Island, NT, Hong Kong SAR, China.
E-mail: proverse@netvigator.com; Web:
www.proversepublishing.com

The right of each writer to be identified as the author of the work(s) that appear with his/her name has been asserted by him/her in accordance with the Copyright, Designs and Patents Act 1988.

Page design by Proverse Hong Kong.
Cover design by Pin-Key Design Co.

All rights reserved.
No part of this publication may be reproduced, stored in a retrieval system, or transmitted, in any form or by any means, electronic, mechanical, photocopying, recording or otherwise, without the prior written permission of the publisher. The book is sold subject to the condition that it shall not, by way of trade or otherwise, be lent, re-sold, hired out or otherwise circulated without the publisher's prior written consent in any form of binding or cover other than that in which it is published and without a similar condition including this condition being imposed on the subsequent owner or purchaser. Please contact Proverse Hong Kong in writing, to request any and all permissions (including but not restricted to republishing, inclusion in anthologies, translation, reading, performance and use as set pieces in examinations and festivals).

**British Library Cataloguing in Publication Data.
A catalogue record for this book is available
from the British Library.**

MESSAGE FROM JACK MAYER
First-prize winner,
International Proverse Poetry Prize (2017)

I am a runner as well as a poet. Running, like writing, is a need, a delight, sometimes painful, often difficult. I've run in marathons with a community of competitors, each of us pounding the pavement for our own particular reasons, or no reason at all. Though awards are given, it's not the gold, silver, or bronze that encourages us at the 26th mile, or running up "Heartbreak Hill." Something more primal, more fundamental encourages our best efforts.

Like running, poetry is a need of the heart. We write in solitude, to satisfy our yearnings, desires, curiosities. Then, with astounding courage, we offer our most profound revelations for others to know, sometimes using competition as a channel. It is a measure of our human impulse to connect with one another that we submit poems to competitions like the Proverse Poetry Prize. We are inspired to edit and revise once again and finally send off our fledglings. And then we run the next mile in our human race, because we have to.

Vermont, USA
January 2019

ACKNOWLEDGEMENTS

All those at Proverse Hong Kong, administrators of the Proverse Poetry Prize (single poems), thank all those who entered for the 2018 competition, and warmly appreciate the helpful and willing participation in the editorial process of those whose poems were selected for this anthology.

We are most grateful, also, for the professionalism and dedication of the judges.

We also acknowledge support from Hong Kong Arts Development Council.

NOTE FROM THE EDITORS
and Proverse Poetry Prize Administrators

For this, the third annual international Proverse Poetry Prize, poems were invited, either on the entrant's own choice of subject or theme, or on a subject selected by the Proverse Poetry Prize Administrators, "Refuge" (interpreted as each entrant might wish). Any form, style or genre could be used.

Poems were judged by the panel of judges as submitted and the following awards were made:

First Prize
Susan Phillips, 'Advancing Dementia'
Second Prize
Thea Biesheuvel, 'Reformation'
Third Prizes
Maria Elena Blanco, 'On reading Baudelaire in the air after a poet's burial'
D. J. Hamilton, 'Why are there Actors?'
Dr Jack Mayer, 'Psalm 23 / Hospice Volunteer'
Hayley Ann Solomon, 'There never was nothing'

Several other entered poems were awarded a place in this International Proverse Poetry Prize Anthology 2018, *Mingled Voices 3*, and their names appear in the Table of Contents as well as on the title page.

Congratulations to all!

Several of the poems in the Anthology were edited by the writers after selection for the Anthology and before publication, but no further judging of the entries was made at this stage.

All writers were invited to contribute a commentary or notes on their poems for this anthology and have responded in different ways.

Brief biographies of those whose work is represented in *Mingled Voices 3* are included in the anthology.

To the extent that those whose poetry is published here tell us about their working lives, we know that among them are editors and literary translators, home-makers, journalists and former journalists, university students (including of creative writing, English literature and psychology), university professors (including of creative-writing, drama, Chinese and comparative literature), expatriate and local teachers of English, translators from French, teachers and translators of the Italian language, a retired biomedical researcher and professor, practising and retired medical General Practitioners, a dentist, a solicitor, a social worker, a former diplomat, a TV presenter, business managers, an educational charity co-ordinator, and the chairman of a Hong Kong Heritage Conservation Project.

Their places of birth are various, and they live in many countries.

Some are new or young writers. Others are already well-published as poets, whether in magazines and journals or in book form. Among them are prize-winning writers and writers who have participated in poetry festivals and other prestigious events; several have many published poetry collections.

Entrants were asked to submit their work in English. To qualify, entries needed to be previously unpublished in English, but could have been previously published in another language.

Most writers chose to enter a poem on a subject or theme of their own choice although some did focus on the subject selected by the Proverse Poetry Prize Administrators, 'Refuge'. Each poem was judged on its own merits and those selected for this anthology are arranged simply in alphabetical order of poets' surnames and (where more than one poem by a single poet is included) also by title (unless a different sequence was requested by a poet). The poets' commentaries and notes on their poems, requested during the editing process, are presented as endnotes. The brief biographies of the poets (which were not known to the judges at the time of judging) appear in alphabetical order of poets' surnames.

Poems were invited in any genre or style. Most, but not all, are in free verse.

THE INTERNATIONAL PROVERSE POETRY PRIZE 2019

We very much hope that all who entered for the 2016, 2017 and 2018 International Proverse Poetry Prize and all whose poems are included here will continue to enter their work in future years. And of course we hope that others will join the competition in 2019.

Receipt of entries for the 2019 competition begins on 7 May 2019 with 30 June 2019 as the deadline.

As in previous years, poets may enter poems either on a subject or theme of their own choice or on the theme suggested by the Administrators for 2019, 'Plastic', interpreted as each poet may wish. (This need not be about plastic bottles in the sea, though it could be. It could be about flexibility as a human physical or spiritual quality. The word "plastic" may be used, but it is not necessary to use it.) Full and updated details will always be available on the Proverse website, proversepublishing.com.

In the meantime, we hope those whose poems are included in the 2018 International Proverse Poetry Prize Anthology will enjoy seeing their and others' work and that all their readers will share the pleasure of the judges and the editors in these "Mingled Voices".

Gillian Bickley and Verner Bickley
Hong Kong

PREFACE

In this third anthology of "Mingled Voices" writers from many lands have again reassuringly confirmed that, where the art of poetry is concerned, there are no national boundaries: poets respond to the eternal preoccupations and feelings common to us all, irrespective of country and culture.

Susan Phillips in 'Advancing Dementia' captures the cloud of confusion in the mind of the dementia sufferer as she struggles to make sense of the shifting identities of herself and her visitor. Her grasp of relationships, and disconcertingly of the sequence of time in her life, has slipped away. There is no sentimentality here but a poignancy in the final anguished plea "Where have you put my daughter? /Have pity, put her back!" Will that plea make any sense to the visitor?

In her poem 'Reformation', Thea Biesheuvel's chosen metaphor of a mighty fortress to represent the image of maternal power is an apt one. Although the aged mother of the family is now constrained within the limits of four walls, she is fortified by the memories of being at the centre and is still the matriarch, still "the keystone of our arc". The metaphor of the fortress is reinforced by the choice of a substantial ten line stanza and its patterns of rhyme.

'On Reading Baudelaire in the Air after a Poet's Burial' shows Maria Elena Blanco moving easily between cultures, religions and languages to express her consternation that Gerhard Kofler, whose *in memoriam* she writes, has passed the barrier and can no longer communicate to the living any answer to the meaning of life and death.

Jack Mayer's 'Psalm 23/ Hospice Volunteer' draws a parallel between the eternal message of hope, so unforgettably and simply expressed in the biblical psalm, and the calming and compassionate work of the carers ministering to those nearing the end of life, bringing comfort not only to the dying but also to "those of us left on the shore ….grazing green pastures to the edge". His six line stanzas are rounded off by a final couplet: "And I am grateful. / You restore my soul."

Hayley Ann Solomon, in 'There never was nothing', rejoices in the Maori myths of creation, sensing that the human mind finds it difficult to contemplate the idea of nothingness from which a creation sprang. Far better to imagine the awakening of the ancestral grandmother looking to the stars, the "thousand jewels of the blanket of night" then the forming of earth's mountains and seas, the brilliant colours of the trees and plants as the forests dance in "bold-blossoming gladness."

D.J. Hamilton's poem 'Why Are There Actors?' seeks an answer to the troubling question of why life becomes unbearable for some unfortunate souls. His compassionate conclusion is that "There is a rain so hard and a wind so cold / that only the laughter of others /might give us shelter." The wound and the dark return with each dawn.

There are so many things here to enjoy. I have room to mention only a few. Steve Borst in 'Boys, I Will Keep You' wants to press as in a book the images of those young boys. The line "Two rabbits not yet heard of the fox" neatly sums up the idea of youthful innocence.

Neil Douglas in 'Enduring Love' gains an endearingly comic effect by the employment of the image of the inquisition and martyrdom in the case of the Brylcreamed antimacassar familiar to wives of a certain age: the offending antimacassar must be boiled, flayed, racked and hung up. Luckily Cupid is on hand in the final couplet to lower the intemperate reaction of fury and restore domestic harmony.

Who can resist Susan Lavender's rollicking tribute, with its rhymes and half rhymes, to Italy through her love of its food? She captures so well the virtues and shortcomings that those of us who love Italy regard with alternate affection and frustration.

Patrick Reardon's poem 'Buttons', in the space of seventeen lines, highlights the great divide between the "Teflon" people interested only in making money and the gardener—he who "hunts stars across the dome of the sky". The closing lines reveal the final irony: the gardener's own daughter could well soon be entering the deserts of those Teflon materialists.

Edward Tiesse, in his 'Tuscan Autumn' reflects, as he walks through the hot dry Tuscan hills on the powerful feeling of a past that is still present permeating the landscape: he hears the voices of those who have lived under the "sun-faded tiled roofs" insisting that they too "worked and drank and loved".

The title of George Watt's 'Snake in Hiding by St Peters Billabong' suggests a rather dangerous ambush for the unwary walker, but there is no danger here: only the pleasure of coming upon the work of the alchemist who reassembled the shattered pieces of an earlier and different work of art. The snake now lives again in the form of a kaleidoscope of bright mosaic.

Readers will no doubt find many more satisfying and enjoyable moments here.

Margaret Clarke,

Translator of *Le Monde tel qu'il sera* (1846) by Émile Souvestre and co-translator with her husband, the author I.F.Clarke, of *Le Dernier Homme* (1805) by Jean-Baptiste François Xavier Cousin De Grainville

Oxfordshire, UK

CONTENTS

Message from Jack Mayer, First Prize Winner in the Proverse Poetry Prize competition 2017 — v
Acknowledgements — vi
Note from the Editors and Proverse Prize Administrators, Gillian and Verner Bickley — vii
Preface by Margaret Clarke — xi

POEMS

Vinita Agrawal	The Last Refuge	3
Arthur Allen	Land Of Darkness, Or Darkness Itself	4
Joy Al-Sofi	Gondwana	5
Joy Al-Sofi	In The Presence	6
Indran Amirthanayagam	Nice	7
Solomon Au Yeung	Snapshots By Heart	9
Solomon Au Yeung	The Cycle Of Life	11
Sui Ping Au Yeung	The Pig Ears Didn't Hear	12
Thea Biesheuvel	Reformation	13
Maria Elena Blanco	Axis Of Silence	15
Maria Elena Blanco	Nightbirds	17
Maria Elena Blanco	On Reading Baudelaire In The Air After A Poet's Burial	19
Maria Elena Blanco	Rambling Digression At Thomas Bernhard's Grave, Grinzing	20
Maria Elena Blanco	Rich Jain Temple, Mumbai	21
Maria Elena Blanco	White-Gloved Poetess	22
Maria Elena Blanco	Writing Out Of No Place	23
Steve Borst	Boys, I Will Keep You	24
Paola Caronni	The Terrarium	25
Josie Chambers	Cell	27
Carol Flake Chapman	No Exit	28
Lauriane Chappé	Facing The Sea	29
Lauriane Chappé	Wandering Feeling	30
Pei-kai Cheng	The Intimations Of Aging	31
Benny Chia	A Love Poem	32
Helen Davis	Refuge	33

Bruce Dodson	Kowloon	34
John Dorrell	This Colour Shall Be Mine	35
Neil Douglas	Empathy For The Devil	37
Neil Douglas	The Transient Intimacy Of London Transport	38
Neil Douglas	The Imposition Of Ashes	39
Neil Douglas	Enduring Love	40
Hasan Erkek	Mermaid	41
Hasan Erkek	Night Train	42
Hilary Faulkner	A Mother's Love	44
Michael Gould	Causing Climate Change	45
Elizabeth Grobler	Farewell Beloved Rover	46
D. J. Hamilton	The Giant	48
D. J. Hamilton	The Hummingbird Sometimes Flies Backwards	49
D. J. Hamilton	Two Letters To Li Ch'ing-chao	51
D. J. Hamilton	Why Are Their Actors?	53
Matthew Harris	Emotional Refuge Sought Against Fettered, Manacled, Yoked Chain	54
Jonathan Hart	Earth, Water, Refuge	55
Steven Harz	Kaleidoscope Heartbeat	57
Kate Hawkins	Rich Powerful Words	58
Kate Hawkins	Stanley Bay	59
Stephen Herman	Pilgrim Of The Screen	60
Antony Huen	Dear J: In The Banyan Forest	61
Jade Hui	Limbo	62
Akin Jeje	Darkest Day (HK)	63
Meghan Kelsey	The Offering	64
Zachary Knox	Depths Below	66
Christos Koukis	The Ugly Side Of History	67
Franz Krabel	Ocean's Dawn	69
Carol Krauss	Barefoot At Age 10	70
Lynda Lambert	Flying Off To Wales	72
Lynda Lambert	Yes! I Sing	73
Susan Lavender	Consumed	74
Susan Lavender	Fowl And Feline	76
Jemima Law	Lies	78
Elbert Lee	Your Refuge	79
Ho Cheung LEE	Receptionist	80
Rachel Leung	Mary-Sue	82

Rachel Leung	Sweet Like A Bao	83
Rachel Leung	The New Americana	84
Rachel Leung	The Seven Hundred And Ninety-six	85
Selena Liang	Sound Refugee	86
Birgit Bunzel Linder	A Heart Unleashed	88
Birgit Bunzel Linder	Translating Your Poetry	89
Belle Ling	Sorry, Sorry	90
J. P. Linstroth	The Crossing	92
Jack Mayer	Blood	94
Jack Mayer	Psalm 23 / Hospice Volunteer	95
Jack Mayer	The God Particle	96
Aya Mohtadi	Confessions Of An Orphan In Fear	97
Lonnie Monka	Nothing Moves	98
Rony Nair	An Actress Dies At A Wedding	99
Rony Nair	Carp	101
Ty Newcomb	Materiality	102
N. Noéll	Emotional Refugee	103
Keith Nunes	You Can Have My Seat	104
Patience O'Neill	Being in Barcelona, Catalonia	105
Jun Pan	Escape—Overture	106
Jun Pan	Escape—Nocturne	107
Jun Pan	Escape—Pastorale	108
Jun Pan	Escape—Cadence	110
Susan Phillips	Advancing Dementia	112
Danny Poon	Not Forgotten	114
Rochelle Potkar	Amber	115
Simona Rackova	Hair by Hair	116
Joanna Radwanska-Williams	Dreams Of Evening	117
Joanna Radwanska-Williams	The Tartness Of Unknowing	118
Patrick Reardon	Buttons	119
Melissa Reed	Listening To Chang'e Read On Mid-Autumn Moon Festival	120
Melissa Reed	Mid-Autumn Moon Festival, Lake Harriet, Linden Hills	121
Melissa Reed	White Clouds, Red Trees	122
Vinni Relwani	Signals	123
Angelo Rizzi	Homo Erectus	124

Angelo Rizzi	I Count The Inert Hours	125
Angelo Rizzi	The Notebook	126
Halil Suat Saraç	Driving My Lips To The Rainclouds	127
Sanja Särman	Schoolyard Memories	128
Sanja Särman	The Burier Of Flowers Lamenting	130
Sanja Särman	The Fog	131
Sanja Särman	The Only Thing	132
José Manuel Sevilla	The Talking Photo	133
Allegra Jostad Silberstein	A Grace Of Light	135
Hayley Ann Solomon	Let This Refuge Sing!	136
Hayley Ann Solomon	My Refuge For A While	137
Hayley Ann Solomon	There Never Was Nothing	138
Laura Solomon	Building Wharf	140
Laura Solomon	The Party	142
Jeddie Sophronius	In The Waves Of Midnight	143
Andrew Sutherland	Dogbite	145
Andrew Sutherland	Five Blessings	146
Andrew Sutherland	Terminal One	147
Abigail Taylor	Alley Cat Detective	149
Luisa Ternau	Abandoned Beauty	150
Luisa Ternau	For So Sweet Is The Sound Of My Lute	151
Luisa Ternau	Seller Of Dreams	153
Edward Tiesse	Tuscan Autumn	155
Roger Uren	The Failure Of Typhoons	157
Peter Verbica	Stain	159
David Vognar	Magic Hell	160
Olga Walló	Poems	162
Anson Wang	Cross	163
Anson Wang	My Jellyend	164
Anson Wang	Ride With A Spider	165
Anson Wang	The Little One And The Sea	166
Giovena Wang Songwenjia	It Was April Fool's Day	167
Bruce Arlen Wasserman	Eight Months In Warsaw	169
George Watt	Snake In Hiding By St Peter's Billabong	171

George Watt	Trying Too Hard	172
George Watt	Why?	173
Richard Westley	Obliquy	174
Elizabeth (Libby) Wong	She Believes	175
Cindy Wyles	Fairy Tales	176
Cindy Wyles	Vanity Fair	177
Anthea Yip	Dragon's Breath / Inspiration	178
Sally Younger	To My Love In A Mysterious Universe	180
Poets' Biographies		183
Editors' Biographies		211
Proverse Hong Kong		215
Poets' Notes and Commentaries		217
Advance Responses		241

POEMS

The Last Refuge

Lions eat deer
Foxes eat rabbits
Birds, insects
insects, plants
And so it goes, the cycle of survival.

Man
Homo Sapiens
the trophic consumer,
somehow at the centre of the web,
throws himself out of this Ferris wheel
on to a bed of thorns,
feeds himself
to the vultures of vices:
Blasphemy, Luxuria, Avarice,
Gluttony, Hubris, Despair, Pride.
And so it goes, the cycle of destruction.

It devours him,
chews him to the bones.
His ashes become food for trees
minerals for rocks.
The last of his flesh,
bread for maggots.

And in the vast silence that follows,
nothingness is air fed with blunders.
The reduction of something to nothing
someone to no one
the final flaw of existence
the last gaffe,
anonymity, the last refuge.

Vinita Agrawal

Land Of Darkness, Or Darkness Itself

Here is the real dream
around which everything is organized.

Silence on the deer-less track and quiet
as hoof-prints in fallen snow
here comes the ghost of my old dog.

He doesn't break the branches where he goes,
    or touch the snow
and there is no path where I project him
like birds he makes a passage of no marks.
In the dream it is known that a child could grasp
that he is saying more than what he is
saying but he came to woods-edge hiddenly and existed only
outside my earshot because he is going to die
they will let him leave. His little ribcage
at the head of the past

beyond mud and shallow water. How to get ashore
and let you sleep well inside the long chase ahead.

        A jewel-like infant
        on a voyage without baggage.

How to become the nerve to throw oneself down
and rise in easy passage and progress forward
across seemingly endless shallows.

It is not writing home (where distance no longer exists) it is
    to be your own father
writing home where you mistaken or not seen
had been waiting all the while / slow as an anchor
turn face in newly risen shadow and ask who comes
here to mourn the living.

Arthur Allen

Gondwana[1]

Another exotic-location trip,
eschewing Wiltshire's famous stones
and jewel-encrusted peacock thrones,
for nature's tectonic, volcanic
metamorphic folded forms
wind-worn weathering
boulders beaten, river-borne
where in this place ancient
continents once formed.

Namibia's UNESCO treasures
a perfect view
of the world's most ancient dunes
petrified, by pyroclastic pressures
stones pounded into sand
heaped once more
on fog-bound shores
by unceasing, surgent seas.

Far inland beyond the coast,
silence like an eagle's scream
rises on Earth's inmost molten thermals
soaring above ancient petroglyphs,
San rock paintings, dinosaur bones
that lived and vanished long
before the lost Garden's
claim to paradise was even formed.

Look closely, the land
itself, the afterbirth of
your mother being born.

Gondwana sky still retains
the stain.

Joy Al-Sofi

In The Presence[2]

Elephants
don't shake the earth
when they walk.

Unseen, by day
their size is sensed
in the absence of light
through landscape.

By night
their steps pass
soundless as the moving wheel
of the Milky Way.

Enter the presence of elephants
a cathedral
    of the real
twin, white spires
    fixed
flesh and bones standing
a living Temple of the Tooth
relics still breathing
in the crosshairs
on its last legs.

Elephants
don't shake the earth
when they
walk.

An elephant shakes
the earth
when it
falls.

Joy Al-Sofi

Nice[3]

This word
nice
has sprouted
in my head
like lice

and I am
bereft
in search
of a more
exact

exacting
description
of taste,
distinguished
finely,

sausage
made by
German
Polish
English

immigrants
to Baltimore
where
Poe
passed

his last
ghoulish
gas on
a street
which may

now house
an eatery
with nice
bangers
and mash.

Indran Armithanayagam

Snapshots By Heart
~~we see by our eyes, but much clearer with our hearts~~

Shutter blinked, Snap!
that moment when the falling leaves kissed the pond
sketching waves of ripples
using a rare silence to warn this repetitive rush
of the crowded crowds
    to let go
the packed shoulders rubbing in such inharmonious squad
    to let go
the dark saturated lumps of metropolitan madness

Shutter blinked, Snap!
that blurry spot right in front of the Triple Lanterns
a shadow overlapped by two
another bundle of strangers' kisses
leaving behind the burden of stigmatized professionalism
    deeply embedded in a camera
appearing nice & clear, an old couple's promise on an
    ancient bridge
bearing this precious moment, so they can live out the
    eternal presence

To grasp by heart that once blurred vision under the shutter
glancing right at the crystal-clear surface underneath the
    bridge
That distant "him", holding up a long-lost smile
slowly taking in this lightness in relief

To grasp by heart yet another blurred vision under the
    shutter
behind the three lanterns, shadows reappearing, flashing
became the typically Chinese revolving lamps, noted
that without the burden bounded by a so-called camera set
catching the shadows only written vaguely in waters
realizing those seemingly familiar blocks are...

wait a second, once our very close
family, teachers & acquaintances?!

Solomon Au-Yeung

***Triple Lanterns is an antique cafe located on the coastline of
the Venice of the East—Tai O, Hong Kong*

The Cycle Of Life
Life is dressed in colourful robes, the top covered with lice.—
Eileen Chang

Living lives of rejuvenated, lives of countless births, life
unstoppable routines, life; an untraceable past, living
only in the mind, living
awakening the fast-asleep,
a mode of self-defense
flaming suddenly
the ukiyo-e,
a voiceless
hymn

look!
the children
are creating their own dance moves
celebrating their lives, a united tribe

look!
the composition of this place
has started to
change...an endless transformation
Another...Cycle of Life

Solomon Au-Yeung

The Pig Ears Didn't Hear

Invisible beer didn't want to leave the glass
Ding ding dong dong

By word of mouth, coldness was made from fermentation secret
Wrinkles of shirt were like curved pig ears, listened to songs secretly
Extension of the last syllable glossed over the aroma of master stock

An unpiloted game machine the bartender was
One dollar per round within three minutes
The Big Brother made infinite noise

A challenge of new beer and old songs next round
Cheers in Thirteen Streets
Ear bones couldn't hold back

The half-man carried water with a light step
His footsteps came back from far and near
Beer bottles were dripping with small raindrops

Echo reached the halfway mark
The bar was back
The pig ears were back too

Su ping Au Yeung

Reformation[4]

A mighty fortress, in her chair
my mother sits, exists
within her room, her square.
She chats about her skin, her hair,
the home she missed
when this became her Unit.
Her unitary state approved,
though she's the keystone of *our* arc.
could never be extracted. She's removed.
The solitary matriarch.

The strength comes from within, her base
our family tree of old,
possession still of her antiques, kind face,
a stubborn faith, foreign Dutch place,
some chairs, bed-end, papers with mould
piled up where they might fit
Things not for use, or not for her
a stack of memories, an image,
a way things never were
while she was still that personage.

Her children's kids provide a cause
of satisfaction, or disdain
their gifts, a 'lekker koekie', the silent pause
when they don't come, the source
of casual pleasure or deep pain
though this she won't admit.
Her photos serve as proof complete
that once she was, had once a life
and house, real bricks and mortar in a street,
was once a valued wife.

As chaff before a breeze she's blown
away from usefulness and roots.
Her house pulled down, her children grown.
Walled off from life, she sits alone
with memories her servants; idly puts
another bouquet near the bed-side phone.

Between the present and those gone she flits;
A mighty fortress once, now just a ruin.
The ancient landscape of her life befits
the castle of a queen deposed too soon.

Thea Biesheuvel

Axis Of Silence[5]

When we had almost reached it
after countless moons
you lashed at it with your flaming ropes
And once again I conjured up a misty breath
entreating
your sweetest words which came to bend the break of silence
which is not that of the lambs,
nor that of doors gently closing
at the passage of lovers or children.

The silence of a howl deep down the body.

The silence of ice melting on my swollen eyes,
or of the rustling boil of water that will soothe
my polyurethane spine.

The silence of a house, which one,
before it catches up with me.

The house of silence,
That in which you are not.

It might be the smog-filled air:
drippings from evil elves
which besiege us, that tunnel
between your body and my shoulder.
Then rather give free rein
to the lung that's trapping you
or take me in your arms
and that's another story:
imaginary, modular
number.

It is not enough
though useful
to know the geometry of the plane.
What matters is the algebra of the double-bed
the cipher of the windowless night,
the bed being one
of night's windows
while the moon is the other,
the moody
rattle-brain moon,
intractable coma
in the quadrature of this circle.

Maria Elena Blanco

Nightbirds
>To the night birds of that New York night,
>Antonio Cisneros, Raúl Barrientos, *in memoriam*

No plaque commemorates the meeting,
or that or any other venue with that name,
a watering hole where three nocturnal birds
uttered ingenious thoughts that were never written
and on occasion read what they would perhaps write.
The last time they descended from a nearby sixth floor,
already well-seasoned with a good Chilean wine,
the poet laureate sang the chronicle
of a native community soon to be extinct,
of animals whose bodies lay lifeless on the beach,
of a few gray-skinned elders, the only wise men
left on the planet. The next-in-line poet used to swing
between the saga of his blond Hungarian lover
and a host of dubious characters that filled his nights:
dancers, third-rate actresses, gunmen.
The then poet-to-be grasped the instant,
carried along her own blank poem,
was the omnipresent juggler
who today reports that:
Latin American bohemia is forever gone
those night birds lost sight of each other
the Hell's Angels no longer frighten as they did
the sixth-floor friend died of AIDS
the new CBGB's lacks soul
the neighborhood is cleaner
literature's plagued with dirty realism
poetry doesn't drink or stay out late
and stopped smoking, a real bore
poet laureates are a thing of the past
even phoenixes drop dead
the new poetic bird-king
is the condor: crowned,
efficient, professional
nothing doing

one must recycle oneself
more or less
less or more

the world is not the same

Maria Elena Blanco

On Reading Baudelaire In The Air
After A Poet's Burial

> Au fond de l'inconnu pour trouver du *nouveau*!
> Charles Baudelaire, *Le Voyage*

To Gerhard Kofler, *in memoriam*

They must have told you it was bitter cold.
Surely they must have mentioned the black cloud
and the sudden hail storm at the very moment when your coffin
was lowered while the poet Schindel recited the Kaddish
after the ubiquitous Catholic requiem
and a couple of profane invocations.
At that point we were a hundred mortals seized with chill
wishing to run away or join you in your grave. The latter
was out of the question since I was flying to New York
the next day. Once in the air, feeling us somehow closer,
I continued to work on my Spanish translation of
The Flowers of Evil.
Though I was in the middle of one of those sonnets
inspired by the voluptuous Jeanne Duval, my mind
wandered out to the last stanza of *The Voyage*,
which you liked to quote during our chats
at the Café Central or Bernhard's Bräunerhof,
to the great mysteries—death and love—
which are perceived with awe in childhood
but elude us as we approach the void.
And you've already mastered them, like God.
But tell me then, the absolute unknown,
or the ultimate novelty under the sun,
what good is it to you, Kofler, if you're no longer able
to pour it into a poem or a kiss?
                      But pardon my presumption
to delve into the abyss that divides us.
I turn to my translations. The next one is *El viaje*.

Maria Elena Blanco

Rambling Digression At Thomas Bernhard's Grave, Grinzing

In keeping with the image the public has of you, Herr Doktor Bernhard, your grave
is rather difficult to find. But once discovered, one is in for quite a surprise.
If we review your life's venues, including your Grandpa's farm in
Ettendorf, the cellar in Lehen, your last living quarters in
Ohlsdorf, or even others' places, like the Wittgenstein
residence or your character Roithamer's Cone,
which boil down to the same, where you
apparently found solace, one notices
a moderate, if not curt, design
conception, a layman's
touch and an
absence of
kitsch. But
your
grave is
the grandest
at the Grinzinger
cemetery, with its baroque
wrought iron cross adorned with
bronze leaves, rosettes and angels,
its little black retable finished in gold
and a stone base densely covered in ivy and
rosebush buttons rivalling with dart-like iron finials
and the monogram of the Holy Name which crowns the
entire funeral edifice. Your own name is nowhere to be seen,
Herr Doktor Bernhard, only perhaps hidden under the ivy or inside
the retable, next to the name of Frau Hedwig Stavianicek, whom you
affectionately used to call "the old hag", and this belated reunion in
death explains and seals for eternity your stance in this respect,
something which in the light of your work was not obvious
at all and, by the same token, confers upon your person
an aspect far removed from the tough, intractable
image with which, ignoring your intricate nature,
deeply Austrian, that is to say, sentimental
and fanciful, the public and you yourself
have chosen to portray your personality.
And thus, for all these reasons, there
is no need to fear that this, your
resting place, might be
the target of grafitti,
vandalism or
petty theft,
amen.
RIP
Maria Elena Blanco

Rich Jain Temple, Mumbai

Barefoot, I put on the third eye, mumbled
the *navkar mantra*, rang the tiny bell
to announce me to the saint, the main one,
while others were being dressed and made up
or prayed to with closed mouth.
Marble, silver and precious stones from Jaipur
contrast with the self-professed material scorn
of these faithful. Nothing new for me, coming
from baroque Catholicism; instead
I bow to their precocious
theory of being.
Seven are its predicates:
in some ways something is
in some ways it is not
in some ways it is and it is not
in some ways it is and it is ineffable
in some ways it is not and it is ineffable
in some ways it is, it is not and it is ineffable
in some ways it is ineffable. I sense
that this sudden wisdom will enlighten
all my daily and virtual lives
without knowing to which God I should
be grateful. Once outside the temple,
I ecumenically mistook
the chauffeur's Krishna for Jesus,
gave a good tip to the shoekeeper and,
far, quite far, from Jainist orthodoxy,
fondled a wish on the elephant's trunk.

Maria Elena Blanco

White-Gloved Poetess
In memoriam Heidi Pataki

I'm dying—you burst out on the phone to your best friend.
It was not your usual hyperbole.
No one believed you. Least of all you.
The true story goes like this: in exchange
for a translation you offered me some precious jewelry
that had been your grandmother's. I declined,
I said I never meant to charge you, it was
the usual exchange between writers.
Hastily, you dropped it in my open bag
at Cafe Schwarzenberg, declared the subject closed.
A bit later, at Kafka's (as befits Viennese café culture)
we read those poems side by side. Hands clad
in lily-white lace, you were radiant,
seemingly happy with the translation
and a fair trade-off. Not long after,
at a posthumous homage to Gerhard Kofler,
we meet again. You are asked
about a future engagement,
I overhear you whisper a tentative yes,
—and then, wistfully, aside: I hope to be....
You weren't.
Suddenly the rumour spread. An over-zealous bard
of recent acquaintance and scant German
runs from clinic to clinic in your search.
Tying very loose ends, he finds you
under your real name (unknown to all but kin),
bitterly alone, cursing your fate, regretful
of your flight from empathy.
He hugs you.
You, who a few months before had waved
a feisty farewell to the dear dead poet
with your bright red kerchief.
You, who knew full well you'd be the next one
when you bequeathed to me in life
your *Oma*'s gold earrings.

Maria Elena Blanco

Writing Out Of No Place
On being and not being
at St. Erhard in Mauer, Vienna.

Well, what can I tell you, Lord, I'm hung over.
Not like you, of course: from drinking.
I missed Mass at noon, but here I barely am,
at five, in church, to write some poetry.
It hailed today, Hail Mary, on St. Joseph's
—my late father's name day, Our Father.
I sure hope he's in heaven, I'd like to go there myself
and visit him—I miss him. At times I think
I see his ghost, O Holy... But it's O.K. Glory be.
St. Patrick's gone—no parade up Fifth Avenue
in Vienna like in the good old days
at high school, St. Francis Xavier Cabrini,
patroness of migrants, Alma Mater.
Hell! hail in Vienna! (hot in Havana, windy
in New York) in March: two, three, four. Halt!
O Lord, these crazy showers and let April in Paris
—was I ever happy in Paris, Notre-Dame.
St. Clotilde was my church there
(posh place for weddings)—I stopped going.
I finally got married (at the Karlskirche),
late as usual, Lord, but better late than...
O God! I guess I won't make it to St. Erhard's
in Mauer to write poetry. I'm still in bed
—hung over, for Chrissake!
But I'll have been there in spirit, Holy Spirit,
I swear—oh! my apologies, Lord.
I confess using poetic license
—you know, playing with words,
basically: lying. But this time, Lord, I'm
—so help me—yours truly. Amen.

Maria Elena Blanco

Boys, I Will Keep You

Boys, I will keep you pressed in this book
For your eyes again, when you return as strangers.
Exhausted warriors!
You can hide here, while the red world is raging.
And wait like undiscovered dinosaurs,
Pressed between the pages of slate.

Under her knowing eye you have grown,
Curious, round eye of the sparrow;
Two hatchlings swimming in a drop
Two pinwheels set before a gale
Two rabbits not yet heard of the fox.

One shaken from watched sleep,
A blue rooster crows at the foot of his bed.
Out his morning window opened wide
He wheels headlong, drunk with the joy of unreason.

One laying claim to all he sees,
Proud warrior, melting in his mother's arms,
He balks at his brother-fashioned roles
Of serf and grazing dinosaur.

In my cellar you can pass the cold season,
Green apples picked in your time of shining.
No greedy hand can reach you here
Where the days of your freedom can turn forever.

Steve Borst

The Terrarium[6]

It rained, and rained again
Inside.
Droplets of mist,
Pings of breath,
Connected.

The water melted,
Evaporated
In the warmth of a perpetual summer.
It left a void,
A possessive adjective hanging there.

Our

Vacuum
Bubble
Ecosystem
Where
The beauty of
A carpet of grass
A garden of blossoms
A collection of miniature plants:
Fern, ivy, creeping fig, African violet
Finally disclosed to me that

Even inside the green illusion
of a sealed glass jar,
Even within the circularity
of the self-sufficient and regenerating environment,
Even in the perfect prelapsarian microcosm
of butterflies and bees
And you and me…

Even despite the affection
The brain chemistry
The elective affinities
And whatever else it was

When your words
Pierced the proudly independent,
Luxuriantly flourishing ecosystem,
The crystal-clear transparency of the cracked glass
    Revealed a perfect stranger.

Paula Caronni

Cell[7]

When she told them she would try to escape,
The others said:
'At least here is safe, warm, dry.'
'If we wait long enough,
Behave well,
Our time for freedom will come around.'

Nevertheless, she did escape.
And was not brought back.

In the years that followed,
As their walls thickened, grew tall,
They imagined her, wandering.
    Huddled tight together, they
Convinced themselves of her folly.
She, outside, stumbled into new traps,
But she had learned the habits of escape.

She found, here and there,
Pathways,
Now and then
A clearing;
Often,
Fine threads of sunlight.

Josie Chambers

No Exit

Where do you run when all the exits are on fire?
It's not like the old days when expatriates
Could commiserate in famous cafés
Maybe write novels while under the influence
These days when we want to get away
From a country that no longer feels like home
We find that the usual retreats are closed
After terrorist attacks or sweltering from heat waves

On London Bridge they were falling down
In Paris listening to music was punished by death
On the Riviera they were mowed down like wheat
On the Ramblas they were fleeing for their lives
On Mexican beaches heads were rolling like dice
In Rome the fountains were going dry, no dolce vita
So what about Canada, eh, which is looking better
Every day, knowing that in the end, ice is better than fire

Most of us can't really afford to move, of course
And what price would we pay for leaving our roots
And all the memories that are locked in the rocks
And the trees and the houses and the gardens
And what about families and friends who hold us
Anchored to this spinning earth, who know us
In a way that we couldn't be known in a new land
So this is how we learn the songs of immigrants

Carol Chapman

Facing The Sea[8]

Facing the sea, to dream
So many broken waves
And distant shores
But here I am, serene
To leave according to the breeze?
A great desire to sail
Beautiful memories
But here I feel so well
I've seen magic places
and beloved faces
But finally I found
Like a haven of peace
The melody of water
Flowing over reefs
And the song of the birds
Disperse my thoughts
I decide to delay
The uncertain journey
Here, everything suits me
And so does this country

L. Chappé

Wandering Feelings[9]
a Sunday in the countryside

Good was the treat, too rich maybe
Elders take a nap at this time, not me
I go to the woods walking on the track
I hear my heart's beating
Suddenly a clearing
The wind and the bees whisper in my ear:
Slow down, stay there.
That's right, just lying on the ground for a break
The grass against my skin, the warm soil in my back
And the sky in front of me
Clouds tell an endless story
I enjoy dreaming, to invent, but soon enough
I don't distinguish here below from up above
Maybe I drank too much? I'm seized by dizziness
The feeling of falling into the emptiness
I close my eyes and sleep is waiting for me
When I wake up, it's darker and a bit chilly
It's late, I guess that they will worry
Quickly, I come down again. Everything seems silent
But when I open the door I find them all there
And in the hearth, there is a big fire
Reassured eyes, a place for me

L. Chappé

The Intimations Of Ageing

Following in the cold wind's wake, the intimations of ageing
Tinge this year's year's-end joys with a hint of melancholy.
Time, that deep river, glides imperceptibly on,
Bearing off passions and partings, bringing limitless expectations.

Hope is the hawser that holds our life's boat in the current
As we wait and wait for a wind to blow from we don't know where;
Then, hoisting our sail, we can sail off to distant waters,
Wandering like the great peng-bird, released from every care.

Rising up early, I read aloud poems of Dongpo,
Then Tai Ji exercises, for this morning I feel energetic.
Glimpsing grey hairs as I'm dressing in front of the mirror,
Does the frosting, I wonder, now cause me to look more distinguished?

Outside the window, the birds' Mozartian warblings
And the blue, distant hills, charming as Jiaxuan's verses:
Is it poem or painting, time's passing show? It is Liniang
Low-humming the garden's multiflorate splendour.

Keener at close of year, cold wind blows in the bare branches,
Fluttering the few dead leaves that cling to their dream of summer.
It has dropped now, and unmistakably, in the distance,
A cloud like a huge bird floats, with its wings outspread.

試譯培凱公賀歲詩霍克思獻醜 牛津2007年1月29日

Pei-kai Cheng
Translated by David Hawkes, 2007/1/29, Oxford

A Love Poem

What about me?
What about me?
You said you love me
You told the world you do
But you'd rather stay away
Than to be with me
You said you love me
But there're ideas
Bigger than you and me
Inside your prison cell
At least you know who you are
Secure in your own belief
That your fight will not be in vain
One day our country will be free
That your sacrifice won't be in vain
But what about me? What about me?
Out there in the night
When it thunders and rains
All that I want
Is to be with you
Safe from the world
And those daily chores
You know history will make you great
One day, beside you, maybe me, too
Our names are tied together forever
They may even build us a statue or two
But out there in the night
When I feel like a woman
All that I want is you

Benny Chia

Refuge

A place of safety
From the drizzled frazzle
The conceits of our eye fearing
Loss of Home, Family, Friend,
For all our days

To be found

Hazy, through worry,
The Marathon ahead
The gargoyle on your shoulder
Whispering strange nothings,
Life flaying—You are stranger

Where to find refuge In the beaches of childhood?
Wave watching And finding God in the sea horses
The sea is now Stranger
In the swell, lies malevolence

Where lies Refuge?
Security in a smile
A place to lie down and stretch
And wake, your world
Not rocked. Your family there,
Free to stay or wander at will

There lies Refuge
Riding the sea horses
Who will gently lay you down

Helen Davis

Kowloon

Third world Casablanca—Chungking Mansions
smell of spices and fried foods
rise from a first-floor farmers market
jewelry on the cheap
watches and cell phones
that might last for a week
... three if you're lucky.

Labyrinth of aisles and warrens
maze of small shops
harried clerks and throngs of customers
newspapers from a world of nations
money changers
edibles of any taste bathed in a light fluorescent
from high noon to midnight.

Edgy, gritty, feel
above all this
some twenty floors of small, one-star hotels
rest stops for immigrants and new arrivals
Lonely Planet tourists
travelers of low means.

The rattle of Mahjong tiles echoes in the air shaft
by a window
that looks out on other rooms the same as mine
the price is right
stay here a day or two at most.

On my way out this early morning
passing still closed shops
the biggest rat I've ever seen.

Bruce Louis Dodson

This Colour Shall Be Mine

This infection took hold when I wasn't paying attention
my hair dip dyed with that orchid tip convention
of post exam rebellion with no hesitation,
I turned to the purple, to female emancipation

there may have been a bag or two or four before,
perhaps cool converses, a folder for lectures, law
was my subject, and I stood out in every class
in purple socks, purple tops, purple jeans on my arse

those cute violet earrings, that pen of bluish red
or a reddish blue, whichever the labelling had said
was now my motif. The one I loved to wear.
this shade is now *my* colour, not just the colour in my hair

I was fine, I was good, I had it under control,
These amaranthine silken hues are funky, that was all
but when I wore a papal sari for aunty Bunty's wedding
that was when my precious niece told me I was turning
        into the lady who only wears purple.

You see I never knew these coloured hues are also a virus
striding across our cultures in independent silence
an infection making us think that we are so unique
in amethyst baju kurungs on our trips to the east

to Penang in a perse tight hanfu in a bar,
or the violaceous hued shalwar for iftar
with just close friends, who never stop complaining
that all of them had noticed I was now changing
        into the woman dresses only in shades of purple.
           Only purple.
              All the bloody time.
So now shall I throw all caution to the winds,
like a nudist on a beach, I know this ain't a sin,
I always will wear lilac to state my identity.
That suffragetteist colour. That colour of royalty

I thought this shade was mine and mine all alone
but then one night when speaking to mami on the phone
she reminisced about the days she'd sit me upon her knee
and the lilac nappies on my butt my amma gave to me

No this colour wasn't mine and maybe never was
it infected me from birth and I wear it now because
it's a curse, it's a sickness, the idea that forever more
I will only dress in different shades of purple.

John Dorell

Empathy For The Devil[10]

With a gentle loving hand apply the
sticking plaster to my flesh wound, doctor
and show me how much you care. Care for me
with an open heart. It's all I ask for
doctor. I am broken. I am broken
and I need you to fix me. Fix me good,
then tell me why, with kind words soft-spoken,
I feel this insistent crying shame. Would
you do that doctor? I expect you could
try to reach out to me, take away this pain,
mend my spirit, doctor. You should. You should
gather shards—piece me together again.
I demand. I command you. Heal my soul.
And I, in return, shall consume you whole.

Neil Douglas
2016

The Transient Intimacy Of London Transport

Seated adjacent in the otherworld of the Underground
at Chancery Lane our knees brush for a millisecond in the hurtling
eardrum numbing clatter-bang of the carriage; a moment found
in the static crackle of your sheer blue nylons grazing

the bland 50% polyester 100% boredom of my grey trousers.
I sit hunched, clenched teeth and fists, eyes closed tight
against the noise and the furious hard eyes of the commuters
with whom we share this deafening coffin and think we might

never share: a joke, a flat white, a sob on the shoulder,
a dream, a trampoline, a litany of words said and unsaid,
a packet of custard creams, a screaming red-faced toddler,
a kiss in a gloomy hallway, a gas bill, a bed.

By Wanstead Flats I sit alone,
as you alight at Leytonstone.

Neil Douglas
2018

The Imposition Of Ashes

The breath of your prayer
on my neck said: remember
you are dust. Open
my lips, my mouth will praise you
and to dust I shall return.

Neil Douglas
2018

Enduring Love[11]

He taps his pipe twice on the mantelpiece,
eases into his favourite wing-backed armchair,
lightly Bryl-creaming the antimacassar

with his sparse white hair as Grandma tuts,
and plots its stained fate—a Reformation Catholic
to be boiled, grey in Persil, on the stove,

flayed on the washboard, wrung through the mangle,
hoisted to the ceiling, hung high on the rack;
the ritual repeated time after time,

until, exhausted, the threadbare cloth
completes its martyrdom by joining the rags
next to the compost under the kitchen sink.

Cupid sits on the airing cupboard, neatly
folded dark eagle wings, a rueful smile
on his lips and lets go a dart from his bow

aimed at the pendant around her neck
which bears the intertwined initials A, V, O,
Armor Vincit Omnium—Love Conquers All.

As the dart hits its mark Cupid whispers from above—
Surrender now, surrender to this long enduring love.

Neil Douglas
2016

Mermaid[12]

Countless snowstorms have passed over me
countless times hail has hit my heart
hills have echoed my cries
hanging on to a gray sky

my cells are dying one by one
because of grief and anger
I'm afraid of disappearing in the town of *kharamees*

Dear Mermaid Ephtalia
go out of the prison of my dreams
let your voice guide me
take me to that land of tales
which is seven storeys down beneath the sea
let's meet on the brink of dream and reality

Touch my wounds with your tenderness
wash my soul in salty waters
do not refrain from sharing your secret
cure me, preparing
for the storm that is about to begin

Hasan Erkek

Night Train

I

Train, a dagger plunged into the heart of the night
penetrates its pitch-black flesh

Train, a snake glittering in the moonlight
embraces its path in endless longing

Train, a ceaseless song, gliding down the rails
reciting the tunnels by heart, carved rhythmically into steel memory

Train, sprinkling its tranquil sorrow over the night
turning its hair grey with the wisdom of the road

II

I pulled the boots of courage right up to my knees
And boarded the train passing through the night

I met passengers with tortuous tales
Laid my hands on their doleful hands

As each city crystallised through the window of the train
Water ran down onto the flowers of my face

I made mirrors of the misted windows of the train
While waiting for my dreams' goals to take shape

III

I tested my heart on the cold rails
At every junction, I switched the tracks towards hope

As lonely and enduring as a road,
I learned to be stoic, like a train in the night

Turning my life into a long track
I went down it by living

IV

Every train is a poem
blending into the dark with its melody
and completing the meaning of the night

Each poem is a train of images
passing along the thin rails of our hearts and minds
searching for a station in our souls

Hasan Erkek

A Mother's Love[13]

This unwanted canker grows inside me,
Taking over my body, slowly eating away,
Some say I should embrace it as my friend,
Accept it as part of me and nurture it,
On a good day this is my goal,
A presence within me to look after,
But when the headaches, the nausea,
The diarrhoea, the fatigue, the hot sweats,
Take over, I cry, get out, go away,
Leave me alone, you are not my friend,
You are a cruel, nasty, enemy,
Ruining my life, I want to end it all.

Then I look towards my wonderful mum,
90 years old and seen so much in her life,
I am enfolded in her warm, loving arms,
She is my rock,
She is my confidante,
She keeps me going,
She understands and sees this horrible
Cancer journey first hand,
Without her love and support I would
Be living in such a dark place.
Every night before we sleep, we hug
As if it could be the last time,
Goodnight mum, Goodnight daughter,
Love you, sweet dreams....

Hilary Faulkner

Causing Climate Change

There are too many people on the planet we inhabit too many
people giving birth too many people on Planet Earth too many
people with mouths to feed too much confusion and too much
greed. What are we thinking when we conceive?

There is not enough space for the human race not enough room
to roam too many people with no place to call home too many
people on the street passing by going who knows where
for who knows why with vacant stares or bearing the evil eye
too many people with the same thing in mind:
to seek their fortune and fame to find.

Things started out well—the age of the dinosaur was swell—
sadly, since then things have soured and gone to hell
not that human life was ever perfect and serene, but today
things have become nightmarish and obscene.

Some fear the end may be near that our planet might implode
given its heavy load with bodies splattered all over the roads
like so much pancake batter on a griddle. Here's a riddle:
why is our sphere so queer, why is it so perverse?

Let's try kicking things into reverse.

Michael Gould

Farewell Beloved Rover
*Dedicated to my father, Victor Emanuel Steenberg,
14 April 1934-12 June 2018*

You had to go, for the call of life's running tide
is a fierce and clear call that cannot be denied.
You left us on a bright day with white clouds flying,
before the joke you promised to tell, that left us crying.

Just like your favourite poem 'Sea Fever' by Masefield
that you loved to recite,
you couldn't ignore the call on a sunny day
that turned into my cold night.
When you sailed away some of my soul's sunshine followed you
and now like the song of Laurika Rauch everything
and my thoughts are tinted blue.

The wind sings a gloomy song and it's your final ship's sail
and me shaking.
Grey mist is on my face, the grey dawn
and my heart are breaking.
You're off on your next voyage, a new fresh start
while leaving behind winter in South Africa and in my heart.

Treasured, wise words, stories, poems and songs you left us
in your memoirs,
precious, special lessons and memories of you transformed
into guiding stars.
When steering through darkness we'll turn
to their light for guidance
and your love will continue to shine in your absence.

Farewell beloved father, you had to go
to the next vagrant gypsy life.
You left in a merry, peaceful way, but your absence
cuts like a knife.
May you enjoy your journey and next adventures
as a cheerful, laughing rover
and may you find quiet, peaceful sleep
and sweet dreams after the long trick's over.

Elizabeth Grobler

The Giant[14]

Ah, Mèimei, the giant said,
I am so happy.
The foreigner has left and
you have come back to us at last.
Let me embrace you.

> *Please Gēgē, said the little sister,*
> *You are squeezing me so tight.*

Don't complain. Be proud
See how strong your big brother has become.

> *But I can't move, said the little sister.*

Don't worry. Big Brother will decide
When you need to come and go.

> *You're squeezing so tight I'm getting dizzy.*
> *I can't think straight.*

I will think for you Mèimei.
After all, we are the same blood.

> *Can't move, can't think, can't breathe ...*

Ah, my little Mèimei, I see you weeping tears of joy.

(And the giant hugged her tighter and closer
and tighter and closer until she disappeared.)

At last, Mèimei,
We are one.

D. J. Hamilton

The Hummingbird Sometimes Flies Backwards.

The hummingbird sometimes flies backwards.
A girl gathering flowers stops
to watch the bird and hums a little
song of her own making
then lifts her skirt to cross the ditch
to the daisies dancing in the breeze.

Red deer rise imperiously
up the torch lit cave walls.
Cave men stare at the paintings.
One moves his spear
making marks in the dirt.

No one is serving chardonnay.

The hunchback hears the girl's song
and sees her thighs and dreams of love and sighs.

A Moslem moon crosses the sky—
her shining face behind a veil of clouds.

Parents playing peek-a-boo weep
with joy at their babies' laughter.

The moon half emerges from the clouds.
Light fills the window and the eyes
of an insomniac thinking of Mozart's
Queen of the Night and the exquisite
curving line of his lover's moonlit torso.

An eager chair awaits her guest.

On the other side of town an old man is drinking beer
and softly playing the accordion
alone in his basement apartment.

A writer at her desk
chin in her hands
is desperate to think of something.

On the other side of the world
dawn washes the dew drenched temple steps.
Inside, a meditating monk
thinks of nothing.

D. J. Hamilton

Two Letters To Li Ch'ing-chao (1080 – 1140 C.E.)

*Li Ch'ing-chao's husband, Chao Ming-Ch'eng, died in 1129.
None of his poems are known to have survived.*

I. Tempest

A vast army of heaven,
wind and rain descend,
limb after limb of old fir surrender.
They pound against my roof.

The long burning fire
has gone out in the stove,
the tide overflows
the high water mark
every stick of driftwood stripped away.
Even the giant snag,
my seat for watching birds
could not resist.

I must leave this place.
At first light,
I hitch the team
and drive my ponies
mile after mile
over broken boughs.

II. Stopping By the Roadside

I cannot but lift my horse's reins,
see a daffodil,
or hold a single teacup,
but mist fills my eyes.

Blossoms at the roadside
become your yellow dressing gown,
the teacup protests,
it belongs beside another.

I cannot but lift my horse's reins
when even the bells on the bridle
call out your name
Ch'ing-chao, Ch'ing-chao, Ch'ing-chao.

D. J. Hamilton

Why Are There Actors?
For Philip Seymour Hoffman, died 2 Feb. 2014 and
Robin Williams, died 11 Aug. 2014

There is a darkness inside some
that no sun, or moon, or candle or
energy efficient fluorescent lamp
may brighten.
Only the blinding light
of public affirmation
reaches that dark corner.

There is a rain so hard and a wind so cold
that only the laughter of others
might give us shelter.

There is a wound so deep
that no medicine may salve it
but applause.

And the wound and the dark
and the rain and the cold
come back
each and every dawn.

D. J. Hamilton

Emotional Refuge Sought Against Fettered, Manacled, Yoked Chain...

Weighing heavily (in perpetuity) no reason can explain
upon innocent scapegoat, whereat internalized pain
endured extant circa nineteen seventy-seven exiting terrain
sans, Methacton High School hard knocks graduate
    academically ill prepared at mercilessly blistering blue vein.
Some conspiratorially malevolent force fast at work
    cranking chronology dial
an extraterrestrial force donning, housing, loosing,
    plying, and trumpeting guile
schmart threadbare stocking chap pet named Lisle.
Damn frightful how years pinwheel into decades
    loathe to accept reality a half century plus ix orbitz
    leaving waked webbing frayed
marked agedly thee jade
did mortal feasting burnt offerings in full laid
abdominal bloating, engorging, and overly ingesting
    hemlock poison eternal peace paid.
"Where fore art those innocent and precious days of youth"?
That rhetorical question continues to resonate
    reverberate within catacombs of my mind
    increasing frequency thinly veiled as faux decoy, I feel
aghast
    how great intervals where in tarred 'n feathered nation
(me unwelcome to standing ovation,
no matter concerned to conserve or ration)
how carefree, lackadaisical, and leisurely days of youth
    disappear in permanent killer vacation.
I daresay satisfactory answers offered das dazed ape
disbelieving ne'er six times decade cheap invisibility crape
adorning disappearing prestidigitation modus operandi to
escape
darkened deathly divine noose hung around my naked neck
nape.

Matthew Harris

Earth, Water, Refuge

1.
The oak is black against the snow
The crow, too, against the cloud
The earth on the bank is dark blood
The water is almost frozen now.

Love comes running like a fox
And darts behind an errant bush
And the green of the hedge is lush
The birdsong echoes on the rocks.

It was time that hid us so
It was not supposed to be that way
The rain and moon chased the day
Till sun and breath had to go.

2.
The wounds opened to the stars
The smell of pus, the church in ruin,

Bones and smoulder, our nails are claws
These hands are beaten in the sun.

3.
The flax was retted, the lint water
Would kill fish in its flush

The floating of our corpses
The rotting of our heads
In river-run: Liffey, Moyola, Amazon.

And you sang Orpheus
As Osiris was carried along.

4.
Matter is brittle, bitter
The roots are in the water

The rain is in the river
The mouth is a cloud

This hill is a spine
The fish grow thirsty.

Jonathan Hart

Kaleidoscope Heartbeat

If you hang around me long enough, or at all,
you learn that I stutter when I speak to you
even though I do my best, but fail, to cover it up.
But what I won't let you know is that
I also stutter when I talk to myself, silently or not,
because I'm uncomfortable with us both.

If you want to know what it looks like inside my brain,
get a dime store kaleidoscope and fill it with
swear words and the frayed edges of a preschool painting,
twist it while holding it up to the light,
and read the monologue that whispers to me
when the lights go down and I try to sleep.

If you want to know what it sounds like in the hollows
of my chest, there is a snare drum heartbeat
that skips more often than I'll admit, but keeps
the rhythm of the footsteps that keep me safely on
this side of a breakdown and a few precarious paces ahead of
whatever has been following me.

Stephen Harz

Rich Powerful Words

Rich powerful words the paper possesses,
It is secretive in its relationship,
Our mind bonds with the blankness,
And our eyes see a space to fill,
The mind relaxes; the paper receives—the words of escapism

Kate Hawkins

Stanley Bay

What do you know sir, what do you know?
About a war that happened long ago?
My father won't tell me, my mother is shy,
And my grandmother left me no clue why.

So what do you know sir, what do you know?
About that war from long ago?
You see my grandfather died in Stanley Bay
And now people remember that very day.

I don't know much sir, I don't know much at all,
My grandmother is silent from the pain of it all.
And so I ask you sir, I ask you what you know,
About that war from so long ago?

Kate Hawkins

Pilgrim Of The Screen[15]
Circa 1890

Shou Hsing   grandfather   manroot
unspoiled pilgrim   have you seen
the absurd   patron spirit with elongated brow

coolly wild with peach and staff in hand
my own hand a sorry vestige of unripe fruit
the fruit of my father   the fig   the apple   the pear

For years I have eaten nothing but bitter seeds
midnights endless   baskets heavy with well-stones
the wells themselves tasteless and without dreams

For years I have searched your face
among the occidental unrelentless

For years I have pilgrimed through tired country
scrambling through underbrush hungry and without sleep

Old stellar deity   wise-one   leader
unpretentious god   teach me to be yourself a link
between two worlds

Make me all three   varied   reborn hopeful

particular in my journey through the numberless screens

White cloud   prophet   stem and leaf
open my eyes the way your eyes open
and close   bring me the fire-blossom from which you

feed and breathe

Stephen Herman

Dear J: In the Banyan Forest[16]
after Deng Fen

we play our Chinese instruments,
yours, guitar-like, mine, flute-like,
without experience or vigilance.

We take refuge in his head:

the gnarled trunks, dangling
and swaying roots,
two plunging cascades—

a virgin forest
in the dissipating mist—

we wear our Chinese robes,
mine, an heirloom, light as lace,
yours, as ivory as the Guanyin statue
grandma worships at dawn,

my hair sticking out from under the hijab-like hat,
your head and face shaved,

your back facing him,
your eyes evergreen.

Antony Huen

Guanyin is a bodhisattva in East Asian Buddhism.

Limbo

the past is a soothing painkiller drug
the present is slipping through my fingers—every second
breeds distance and
the future is aggressively banging on a locked door

we tend not to think about
how entertainers live in cages
how many people are paid to listen to us
how cruel it is to give birth to the dying

yet in the midst of misery we ask
"why me?"

I know what I'm capable of
but I'm tired of trying to prove myself
I wish they would just believe me
I wish I didn't have to
try
so
hard

55% of me is made up of water
and they want to roam free and exit this living corpse

I wanted to drown myself
so I stayed at the bottom of the pool
and prayed my wrinkles would turn into gills

I wanted to drown myself
so I poured burning liquid down my throat
smiled and reassured others that it's just a hobby

I wanted to drown myself
because you no longer guarded my life

Jade Hui

Darkest Day Hong Kong

1. The span between the cold void of night and morning's first glimmer, volcanic glass dark with a streak of shimmer, is longest on earth's darkest day.

2. The span between hope and change to make this deeply
    riven nation inflate again is deepest between shining crests and lightless troughs as it twists and contorts through showers and gusts.

3. The distance between what enlightens us and the spectres that frighten us has created a delirium of spasms chasms so fathomless even adamantine determination to bridge and to bridge these lividly trembling schisms bends and frays.

4. The breadth between a black child's first breath and last breath is often, like December 21st, the shortest of days. It is no accident that darkness falls sharply, suddenly like that day.

5. Hong Kong has yet to see its darkest day. May the powers that will be soften their stance so that this aromatic harbour can remain this way.

6. I told my toddler son in the night just before the dawn, baby I'll be damned if you'll be left in the shadows.
Awake, my sweet little boy—stretch out, stand upright.
We will stride forth together, through the deep blank chill,
Into the brilliance of the light.

Akin Jeje

The Offering

Inside the temple of the million telescopes I give coins to the guardian
of The Year of the Rabbit, & under hanging vines in the park
a blockbuster is being filmed. The actor looks familiar—
the blessed god of self.

I stop to see that every woman is shaped like a flame;
and so—to appear like a precious emerald—don't say green card.
Pretend a trellis is the name of a city we lived in,
Add peeled ginger to sweeten the steel roots underneath
the concrete of what was made last night.

I try soursop and learn it's an evergreen.
Ponderosa Pines grow out of my palm—you seem lost there.
I understood my life had become a prescribed burn.

I met you waiting tables & making simple syrup:
Many times I watched your knife slice the belly of a fish.
To place you in China with me & then take you out of China,
To place you in filaments of distant fruit & eat.

A woman makes paper carnations & it reminds me of doubt,
How each fold makes the flower more life-like;
Your sister had a baby back in Japan—it was born too early—
& to understand desire you'd watch me at table nine explaining sake
& the fluctuating prices of wagyu in the Summer,
How it costs you and then doesn't cost so much.

I've never regretted doing a kind thing for you I've told
myself over & over.
The tabloids mostly wrote of monks and tigers
and how the monks sold them for money, and the
palmistry ads were blown away—fate sealed to a bench
by the rain.

Your grandfather raised chickens on the roof of your
family home;
He and the chickens died in a fire but that was long before
I briefly called you mine

Meghan Kelsey

Depths Below

high off reason
drunk off I told you SOs

i sink and drown in the shallows
of everything i think i know
just another lost soul in the
sea of faces that wanders in
search of what direction to go

drifting without aid we suffocate
bumping into each other like debris
in crowded public places
where each smile
each water-logged apology
seems to mock me

it's then and there in that moment
of epiphany, i find the need to cure
everything i've so far done by fire
once more to be overwhelmed by
the desire to break free and run in
the bright yellow rays of the morning
sun

it's in this moment i don't feel the
endless stare of everything that's wrong
with me and i'm naked and unaware
that to be means to be and once more
feel as reckless as i did when i was
twenty

Zachary Knox

The Ugly Side Of History[17]

Johnny took everything he had, there was room for
everything he had in one wind anyway and came to the
capital
What else can
a white boy do
but write
poetry to
manifest in
the minds of
men

and one day when I took him home wounded,
he said one evening
I will tell you about the ugly side of history

Andreas was in trouble and could not be
saved even by a drop of blood he
packed up and went to his village
but pain never disappears; it is simply
archived
and he wanted to dream like everybody else on the
bright side of the moon

and one night when I treated him to many drinks, he
said
one evening I will tell you about the ugly side
of history

Aalen woke up sweating over a dream
she had walked places that were erased
and roads that never existed and she
kept thinking: people like us change the
world
with a song or a glance

and one day when I brought her medicine, she
said
one evening I will tell you about the ugly side
of history

Angelos always wanted
another body, not his own
he paid every day for the stupidity
and the perversion of the world but
he knew very well that love was an
unlikely reality
and the most beautiful terror is to love
yourself

and one day when I saved
him from his parents, he said
one evening I will tell you
about the ugly side of history

Kat had gone through illegality; she had already
gone through boredom
and was always searching for a new activity, a
new collision
as she was beautiful and rich,
everything legal was too easy
Besides Paradise has a taste of
failure, which is also its value

Kat had somewhere, somehow
thrown her microcosm on a pile
and one day that I remained silent so she
could cry correctly, she said one evening
I will tell you about the ugly side of
history

With these people
I had always the
shocking feeling
that I was not right

Christos Koukis

Ocean's Dawn
For my mother, who died of cancer.

The world turns still, though the light is gone;
Devoured in the maw of the scourge of all.
The birds still sing, the day dwindles on,
The seagulls in the sky scream and call.

As still in death as she was vibrant in life,
Her eyes closed, to sleep one last time.
The silence beheld on the edge of a knife,
The bells give one last mournful chime.

The fire burns fast and bright,
Though not as bright as she,
A pale parody of the light
That moved and set her free.

The sky of the past is bright;
The dawn of the present aflame.
But even the sun sets into night.
And the world will not be the same.

For upon this last great dawn;
The last she'll ever know.
The air's filled with the ocean's song,
And the whole world's aglow.

The wind picks up; the ashes spin,
The great seas call her forth.
Her spirit swims to the depths within,
Her ship has at last found berth.

She was born upon the sea,
Amidst the salt and spray
She left the ocean to be free
But to always return, one day.

Franz Krabel

Barefoot At Age 10[18]

I take the desire path from the slamming kitchen door

    to the geometry-straight vegetable garden.   Bee balm, thyme, thorny blackberry.

Squash.

The swingset next door dry heaving,   filaments of sound

    threading to my ear's labyrinth.   The woman sprinting down

        Greenbrier Road.

Cows and pigs on her pink pajamas.   Her rogue Jack Russell

    dog-gnawed through his leash.   Flashes of his belly, frog-throat white.

        Foot a fix.

    An errant buzzard feeding off the suet seed, as

        seagulls cloverleaf.

    Trilling in delight at the closeness of the devil's dance.   Cadaver kisses.

    Cow's path. A cut through.   Where the heart really wants to venture.

I was saddled with corrective shoes until aged nine.

                Blocks of brown unbending

     restraints. Under the bed. In the closet. Beneath grass stained dungarees.

                never on my
                          feet.

No straight and narrow.   A shortcut.   Nothing as

tempting

                              as a desired
                        path.

Laces loose.

Carol Krauss

Flying Off To Wales[19]
With appreciation to Dr. Ann Paton, for inspiration sent to the author via E-mail from which I created this found poem.

Tomorrow
I'll be flying off to Wales
for vacation in our usual place,

What do we do there?

Walk the coastal path
or sometimes
just gaze at the sea
read
nap
revisit old friends.

Attend choral evensong
at cathedral every evening
read
nap
For us, that's an ideal vacation.

St. David's is an ancient village,
the cathedral
a holy place
where prayer has been read daily
for over a thousand years!

Lynda Lambert

"Yes! I Sing"[20]

Accumulations of summer dreams awaken flamboyant
Baroque memories at twilight.
Constellated time peels off thin layers.
Done!
Erasures revealed endless
fabrications
garnered in dusty corners among
hushed vowels and
illuminated adjectives.
Joyfully, I count my verbal
keepsakes—a lengthy
List of favourite words.
Muse of my Summer Solstice
never tolerated
obscure nouns. I often reflect on
perpetual
queries of long-forgotten
red roses or gifts from a distant
summertime.
Timelessness remains an illusion
until liturgical prayers begin at
Vespers.
Warm voices sing—always In Greek,
Xenia, reminds me, "Be generous."
Yes! I sing a litany of summer's chords,
Zeitgeist notations of my serpentine years.

Lynda Lambert

Consumed[21]

There's a pretty place and it's quite far….
But why the third person? You know where you are!

Your espresso's *corretto,* your parmesan cheese
Brings me to my knees.
Your pasta's divine—
Especially paired with your wine!
Your *tiramisù* is to sigh for, your *gelato*'s to die for.
Your *tortelli* are *belli,* your *maccheroni* are *buoni.*
Your *Napoletana*'s world heritage,
Your Prosecco is vintage.
In the kitchen you're supreme.
That's a fact. You know what I mean.

But is that enough
To put up with all your other stuff?

You strangled me in red tape,
From which I could not escape.
It was more *al dente* than your spaghetti,
When they are cooked just "*perfetti.*"
You put me through a sieve of your rules,
Making my eyes swim in soup pools,
Then you baked me, like sauce,
Between the layers
Of your incomprehensible *lasagne* of legislation
From which there is no recourse,
Only annihilation,
Because you have no remorse,
Just paragraph upon paragraph
Without full stops, commas or verbs,
Which deep-fried my nerves.
So you marinated me in my own tears
And left me there for years and years….
Before making a pizza with my brain
And pouring my blood into it to drain,
Pierced by the vinegar-soaked capers
Of your forms and formalities,
Smothered by the mozzarella

Of your paperwork's illogical banalities,
Not to mention the statutory delays of those anchovies!
Tied down by the tangled tentacles
Of your grapevine bureaucracy,
In the end you ate me
And the few crumbs of my humanity
That remained on your plate, on the prescribed date,
You put in a blender and mailed back to sender,
Pureed, sanitised and finally… lobotomised.

So now, oh my Italy, this is the result you see:
Re-educated by brainwash—
In a perfect *cappuccino* froth—
Despite our feud
And your Kafkaesque moods and vicissitudes,
I still love your food!

Susan Lavender

Fowl And Feline[22]

It was 1995, Valentine's Day.
Lantau was still an island; D.B. still a real bay.
You could only travel to Hong Kong by ferry
And 1997 was not just a local but also an expat worry.
There were still two years left,
Though passing at an alarming rate,
When I heard a Valentine lovebird and his beloved mammal
Ponder their post-Handover fate.

The proverbial Owl and Pussycat sat side by side each day,
As the 7.20 pea green ferry left the Bay,
Same seats, in silence or in speech; always together,
Though by no means birds of a feather!
Two remittance hippies, turned 40, living broken expat lives:
They were two of a kind—
Though more different species it would be hard to find!
Knowing England as those who do not *only* know her,
Surviving, just a little longer,
In the setting sunlight of our Harbour,
She knew the inside of his head,
Like the lines on his face,
Without need to hear his voice nor his features trace.

She'd listen to his colonial ramblings from the past:
"*When I was in Brunei….*"
To which she'd smile and quietly sigh.
The progress of the Blackburn Rovers,
The latest cricket score…and more and more….
They'd laugh together at unspoken jokes,
Complain about the crossword clues,
Recalling their sixties salad days,
Sharing the same youth, same age, same muse,
But this time they faced the future
And counted down their nineties final days,
In this borrowed time and place,
This goose that laid the golden egg, this tiny special space!
Their contracts ending, China coming,
Where could they go? They had no crops to sow,
Nowhere left to roam. Home?

After all this time **_Hong Kong was_** home.

Family? No sister or brother. They only had each other.
So they planned their last bid for freedom,
To end their glorious final season.
"We won't go back," they vowed *"when we're sent home,*
Won't be extinguished without reason."
She pointed out a little sampan
They might stow away on tomorrow,
Wearing the red and white spotted handkerchiefs
he'd buy for them today—or somewhere borrow!

But *The Owl and the Pussycat* is just a nursery rhyme.
The Shape of Water's no more than a fantasy.
Like Cinderella and her prince,
They were simply out of borrowed time.
In reality different species cannot mate
And they could never be
More than just a fairytale Valentine date.
They would never be a couple
For theirs were ties that could not forever bind.
She would never share his bed
Though she'll always share his mind.
So there would be no honey,
No more plenty of money,
No love song for this Owl to sing,
For his Pussycat no ring.
There'd be no dance by the light of the moon.
These two endangered species would be extinct very soon.
Their flotsam colours still sticking firmly to the mast
Would be the only remnant symbol left floating of their past
When 1997 shipwrecked and exiled them,
Each on a different shore,
And daily ferry rides to Hong Kong,
With Valentine pipe dream wishes, were no more.

Susan Lavender

Lies[23]

We are about a body width apart
yet our minds are galaxies away
I'm close enough to see the small freckles
on your neck yet I can't muster up
the courage to ask about your day.

I guess I'll have it that way.

Here next to you I don't say a word
My vision is blurred, my speaking is slurred
A tornado in my head, my thoughts are stirred
but I look calmly at you.

When you're near me I can't breathe—I need to be freed
But yet when you speak I have all the air I need
Your presence surrounds me in a familiar embrace
All the sleepless nights are suddenly erased

and I feel misplaced.

Shattered glass cuts me slowly and painfully
silently killing me
these are what your lies are doing to me.

Jemima Law

Your Refuge[24]

your refuge	an eight headed gargoyle in nascence
an ever expanding physical space	it declared:
overlooking horizons	therefore, you loved your work and aquaintances
you liked the climate control	and the plentitude of betrayals
and the many parties to hold	your company—a feast unremovable—abysmal
an eight faced goddess seeking alliance	my refuge
at harrowing times	turning into contours of undulating presence
you banned the climate control	therefore, tomorrow is not promised
upsetting the pillows	what are now vacant—a feast unstoppable—faith
your body	evolving sacred space

Elbert Lee

Receptionist[25]

The clothed table had just been moved outside.
I followed, seated, like a ghost.

I scanned the objects on the cold white
surface as in a crime scene and found the

two vases imbalanced. A small piece of the
plastic orchid had to go next to the frame.

Mulinda had asked when the picture was taken
and that was the only question I had.

All envelopes came tidier than expected—
all names readable and so I only needed

to care about the cash—from 301 to 10,001,
that's how Chinese people use odd numbers

to avoid double misfortunes,
though I had a few 50s, Canadian dollars.

Canadians are more immune to curses.
I handed over the programme, the white packet,

avoiding thank-yous, the guy had advised,
we said *you are so thoughtful*, as I did to some

six groups of people in an autopilot mode.
The drawer full of black ribbons we didn't touch;

a take-away menu from a nearby restaurant;
and a dozen empty packets with a different cover.

The choking smell of lily dimmed the corridor—
people all came with a film of smoky silk swaying

after them like a wedding gown in a neurotic wind.
The effect was nearly acoustic, a timely prelude

to Massenet's Meditation to be played by my brother.
Oh yes, that was his wedding

when the picture was taken,
when she was only 85 years young.

Ready in ten minutes. I took the bag
inside as the men stopped coming out.

I sat alone in the front.
My cellphone screen reflected

someone who evaded my eyes.

Lee Ho Cheung

Mary-Sue

here lies i,
perfunctory glorified
ascetic white-laden
flawless paper maiden

and me, so bitter,
i chew my own bones for dinner
the rebel didactic mystique
femme hitler sympathique

think not otherwise,
want not, reprise her demise,
so was her and her before her
to grace recluse, for the true debonair.

swim with cold fish, or
else lash out and be a pretty airhead whore,
spit, spit out black feelings.
content to drown in fractured glass ceilings.

ask me why i'm so confused
how the hell i managed to lose
my soul in his cologne—
go,
puppet show
John Doe, Monroe.

Leung Rachel Ka Yin

Sweet Like A Bao
by Leung Rachel Ka Yin

Your voice sounds like the red of a lampshade
at the wet market
like the flopping of fish on the chopping block
like swearing taxi drivers
like a leaky AC unit, like the innards of a
too-hot dimsum, like a stray cat meowing,
a chow-mein being chowed
a truck mixing concrete
a canton opera at the Central Pier.
Like an Octopus card beep,
like a plethora of neon light boxes
like pergolas in the park,
a chestnut shell, an MTR crowd
when the doors are closing
like the speed meter on a red minibus
like Char Siu Bao,
an old-style cash register, like a million
Mark Six balls being scrambled, like someone
trying to sub-divide a flat,
the opening jingle of a TV documentary three doors down,
a really uninteresting PSA on Radio One,
the sound of a waiter when someone is slow to order,
like durians being opened on a rock
like a whole housing estate airing out their dirty laundry
on a Monday, like an enthusiastic beginner
shuffling the Mahjong tiles, like Cha Chaan Teng,
like 7 oranges rolling down the slope
like 5 pickpockets pickpocketing
like the sound I heard when having an afternoon sleep
and someone tried to tune the piano.

Leung Rachel Ka Yin

The New Americana: *then wear the gold hat*

love, sing me a daisy, a fistful a penny
rain fever sweet in your riotous twenties
star-spangled, light-speckled, glitter aplenty

love, sing me a maqam* and i promise to cry
you tears of black gold, till you will have me, high
on your stones, breathe in my bones, my bones, bone-dry.

you had your lush, lush rush, your roaring nights
of brazen swirling silken shirts, wet, stretched tight
over my heart of cold, vulgar, veblen-esque delight

and i, since you have left, have been scratching at it
a scab—a little, jaded, cynical something unfit to skip to stop,
buried deep in greenback kisses

love, sing me a song—anything—
drown me in my pool of roses, of glimmering silver rings,
in your voice full of money, of snapped fairy wings

ain't it a kitschy world, love, all that glitters is not gold.
just like me, look closely,
guldet blev til sand.

Leung Rachel Ka Yin

maqam: the system of melodic modes used in traditional Arabic music
guldet blev til sand: Swedish, "gold turned into sand", from the musical, Kristina från Duvemåla (1995).

The Seven Hundred And Ninety-Six

who will vindicate us, the illegitimate?
the born, the alive, flailing, with wizened limbs,
with our white-capped heads hidden under bonnets, hidden
from sight, only wanted until we are
born.

send help,
the good help,
the good help to help us go
from womb to tomb
to tomb but
not even a tomb.

we envy our unborn brethren.
they turn in their wombs, their gestation a sacrament
denied us in living and we cry
for our mothers, mothers, mothers,
our fathers disavowed
of us and
we turn in our tomb but it's
not even a tomb.

tell us, tell us our bones,
where we are to go
to save us the suffering of being
birthed
birthed into a world
that is adamant on our birth then
washes its hands of us.

Leung Rachel Ka Yin

Sound Refugee[26]

I probe deeper
into the echoes, of
my ears

Stuck
in plastic
sound gears

Where are you now?

The transit dance without tears
transient news
of cheers

Under the ground
Under the ground

The darkness's running wild outside of me

Hopeless to shelter
alter the commuter
dear

I'm faded

The sea-wet rock
never solid and aged
once staged

a solitude that rocks

The King of Karaoke sings in haze—
Please don't frown
if my singing
is not touching
enough

Where are you now?

You snore
in this rhymed non-rhythmic

Pathetic

Selena Liang

A Heart Unleashed

A bird far, far away
was spotted in the dimming sky.
It flew back and forth,
and when it came near,
I saw it tumbling in the air.
I pointed at trees for it to perch,
but its wings would not obey.
I called the crows for help,
but the bird laughed at their black foray.
I built a shelter for the coldest night,
but it rather danced on the antennas above.
At dusk, it sang past the last tune,
and at dawn, it still sailed in song.
When the sky brightened,
I stood with empty hands
and called it by no name.
Then it came near for me to see,
and I saw the bird
was my own heart
outside of me.

Birgit Bunzel Linder

Translating Your Poetry

i got lost in the forest of fallow words.
where the trees sigh when clouds white them out;
where twigs stretch their fingers toward the birds;
where memories perch in old steps, and
where leaves dispatch inscriptions into the earth;
where moss becomes a mirror between crown and root;
where deer fear the black antlers of the wintered chestnut tree;
where foxes leak their colour into autumn undergrowth;
where the woods border on water, and
bones grow into glassy skin
that in the early morning breathes
under the first ballet of the dancing water bug.
when i look up, i am in your homeland
a land that once was my home, too.
echoes of words swing everywhere,
not from the voices of our prophets,
but from the mysterious creed nature narrates.
in my forest, dervishes dance and recite,
and angels waive my paucities left and right.
in your forest, a single leaf falls onto my shoulder
and slows my gait.
i watch the clear and cool rain conquer obstacles, and
i see my worlds confined in heart-shaped drops
that hang suspended from green leaves.
i measure my steps and walk backwards
to collect the breadcrumbs of lost memories
until in the clearing, the same majestic tree
that rooted me as a child, shelters me again.

Birgit Bunzel Linder

Sorry, Sorry

                Two ducks spill over
                     a bowl of rays, the gold feels morose

                         in the pond's mud. These two self-
mesmerizing ducks dip the day,

      tilt to bite the sun and drop its oval,
                binding the rumbaed rhombuses,

          and any straying lights
                 to their flanks. They speak in tongues.

        They stop—
like a truncated future, saying:

              nothing will be explained.
      They drill and wheel and flag their beaks;

    their eyes are slits, their minds are pores.
                    They belittle anything big.

            They smirk at the sun's
        kinetics by shaking.

              There are days like this:
                        just this me seeing—

    what comes before and what ruminates after.
                That buoyancy,

    being a part of everything around,
is a skyward bandage,

        a sheen's week-long peeling
      on a square foot of the pond,

       the *no no no*, so fluid and substantial

          in the middle of an explanation,

a pallid apology, which, once pierced by fear,

    is mistaken for an evasion,
        like the existential *sorry*,

the laborious *sorry,*
    that leads you nowhere but to face the wound.

Belle Ling

The Crossing[27]

Across stark ravines and arroyos…
They crossed the Sonora…

They were three plus their coyote…
Organ pipe cacti stood tall in blue shadows…
As if hidden men staring at them…
They crossed…

It was very, very dark with the exception of a lantern moon…
Its orb some enormous fish's eye in the great deep…
Illuming depths of a fathomless ocean in the
    pitch blackness…
Winking in and out of thin clouds crossing the dark skies…

Along a worn sandy path, they encountered a woman and
    her child…

They shared a cantina of tepid water…
And if you could see their faces, you would see
    their desperation…
But their faces were black in the shadows…
And even in the cold desert night, they were sweating…

Of a sudden there was a helicopter overhead…
Irradiating the organ pipe cacti and the sage brush
    and the sand…
And this great light searched them out…

This light like a great illumined eye found them…
As they were caught by the great beam…
They began running in all directions, panicked and scared…
Like lizards scurrying toward the shade of rocks in
    a beaming sun…
And yet hiding from a raptor's eye of some maniacal mechanical
    immense eagle…

From a distance, headlights also could be seen,
    coming toward them…

Converging on them in three directions…
Kicking up dust in the beams…

Six shafts of light moving up and down…
With the rusty dust wafting into the night air…
As organ pipe cacti and sage brush illumed…
Throwing haphazard shadows in the cold desert night…

J. P. Linstroth

Blood—House-call On The Canadian Border[28]

After three days hard snow,
this border town is ominously picturesque.
My snow boots break a path
to seven-year-old Rodney,
who lives in the Charbonneau trailer,
completely drifted over on Troy Street.
The Alberta Clipper's arctic blast
across the Canadian border
whips my face, whips windows wrapped in plastic,
scatters heat like feathers shook loose
from geese too lame to migrate.

The steel of my stethoscope is a shock
on Rodney's chest. His blue-rimmed eyes widen,
his breath sucks in, and in again.
I search for shine in his too-heavy eyes.
What does Rodney know of radiance?
Through my black stethoscope
polar winds search empty caves for blood.
I must believe that his heart still pumps the energy of creation;
possibility still suffuses the capillary network of his dreams.
But Rodney wears sneakers in the snow
and sleeps beside the gas stove
that bakes warmth all night to save on fuel oil.
He'll grow a few more winters
and lose his one-eyed teddy bear.

School is cancelled,
the street muffled by snow.
Until it melts.

Jack Mayer

Psalm 23 / Hospice Volunteer

You move through this realm of not quite
reality, not quite illusion,
like a song of praise from the shepherd
saying, "you shall not want," to those on the journey,
and to those of us left on the shore,
our flock, grazing green pastures to the edge.

In the still waters you wash the feet of those
about to enter the valley of mystery
where there are no shoes.
You remind us of the table still set before us,
our cup overflowing gratitude, the restless soul
seeking mercy, comfort.

In the shadow of the valley of fear,
long named as evil,
your sweet song transforms darkness into twilight.
You sing the blessings,
your presence anoints the paths of righteousness
with a warm heart.

Can there be a more graceful gift
than to shine light in the darkest of corners,
to bless what has been, and be born
into what always is.
Lessons for living
in the house of the Lord forever.

And I am grateful.
You restore my soul.

Jack Mayer

The God Particle

When I hike Vermont's Long Trail, I compose a poem and leave it at a shelter under my trail name, "Mountain Poet." I left this poem at the Clarendon Shelter.

They found the Higgs-boson!
Physicists call it the "God" particle,
detected by Hadron Super-Collider
atomic smash-ups
releasing a galaxy of particles and,
in a Galileo moment,
fleeting evidence of the Higgs-boson.

Near as I understand,
the Higgs-boson tells us we have mass,
we are real.
Now we have to dig deeper into the mysteries—
hew a bit closer to our next incarnation of God.
Perhaps the Higgs-boson will explain the Law of Gravity,
the law we are meant to defy from birth to death.

Tomorrow night the full moon will hang in the sky
and arc the night.
Fireflies will blink with fierce fluorescence.

Robert Frost said it well—
"We dance round in a ring and suppose,
but the Secret sits in the middle and knows."

Jack Mayer

Confessions Of An Orphan In Fear

In a flash of mere seconds,
I come to you,
a refugee.
You,
a refuge.
I am nothing but a child,
orphaned and afraid.
You look at me, a stray,
and I am not an orphan anymore.
You hold me—like a mother—with fear,
and I am not afraid anymore.
May these seconds last forever
And forever be a flash.
Time dies
And there remains
The truth;
"I love you."

Aya Mohtadi

Nothing Moves

    nothing is not nothing

    *

    refuse to live on the line
    where future projections become
    passing flights of the imagination:
    where everything is possible
& nothing actually happens

    *

    regardless of religion
    no one should worship nothing

    *

    if everything always moves
    then nothing stands still

    *

    nothing is not natural

Lonnie Monka

An Actress dies At A Wedding[29]

One by one they pass away
leaving you and me, apart in tether.
measuring gauges of feeling once imbued.
weighed hold-alls. brimming. imaginary indents. Edges
    fudged.

Love was a clasp from the back you said,
 'when the actress feigned a no, she actually meant yes.'

Old stories from long ago. Old stories, from knee deep
    dusks.

One by one we vanish within ourselves.
hours broken, hours spent. breaking gender, breaking bread.

The actress drank to excess, drank to fade.
Designers Wedded her new couture, Wedded her bills.
Actresses play at plastic wile, between real takes of reel
She took multiple holidays, oral gutters. trashing bloodfins.
imagined tie-ins.
Silence. In bathtub death.

Again, we return. To You and me.
We ran at firth heads, you hurled four letter curses.
I pick up phones to hear your fisherwoman scream
I pick up phones to hear filth spewing. The actress. A
    1990s' reel.

One by one our days recede. Breaking up memory—into
    piecemeal.
Spaced out, fixed door odometer spins, re-runs in old pirouette.
Sparse seconds tumble like dry riverbeds,
Orifices draped red with rage.

Behind those fickle pigments,
your cheeks always flush.
A pair of snatched out fingerprints,
There used to be us.

Actresses die at Weddings.
We died before us!

Rony Nair

Carp

Canonization gives one escape—the spare end of the wheel,
spinning around, its rigmarole a mirror

in reverse. ejaculating dogma into your mind,
staking out one's own. beggar bowls of pity

plying death, in parabolic hoops of long ago pastiche, replaying reels
in fast rewind. death.be kind

over thee and without. projectiles spin over rough shard
curve balls, thrown out—final rounds.

You're our newest anointment,
I'm the stately grope on the same page—squeezing memory,
through sluice sheds.
Cowards scream about why they lost, how we won!

Years of reinvention—carve out newer truths. Years of
　　　reinvention
Tie up the same old stories—alternate junctions in meander.
Land's End.

All endings begin—in wasted confession bins.
all lies bolstered, re-grouped, reordered in multiples. Leading
on towards

Newer causes we outrun. weighed down victims. trains that
await to authenticate circles
 of departures, overflowing into

miracles spent,
gauging each other's tenements.

Rony Nair

Materiality

Proffer me a deal
that I can run-away with.

I want to wrestle in the yards of
the men who were
my father images.

Oh,
but a crowd
would gather,
and I will have to
say profound things about

that old family dream dictionary
with all the animal entries
highlighted. Then,

I'll have to speak about the compact shelf
we kept it on and how it was refurbished
into a coffee table, which

caused everything from
bone-bruised shins to aneurysms.

Ty Newcomb

Emotional Refugee[30]

I never thought I would come this far
when I opened this iron door
I smelled the sweetness of fruits,
the potency and aroma wrapped around me
you smiled and handed me some tools
come work for me, you said

Joining your side was easy
it only required an insatiable thirst
for any delicious and delicate thing.
I was given a new name, a new title
you worked me hard and taught me
to have a voracious appetite

You see me as maggots
writhing through rotting food
you toss me more and more crumbs.
Don't forget your identity, you remind me
I am not just any refugee
I am an emotional refugee

But I am a man with a pliable nature
working hard above my humble station
you cannot read any sullen disposition
certainly not a trace of Machiavellianism
I hide it well, so you cannot tell

I have faithfully served you and this land,
our land, in meticulous and devious ways
the way you demanded that I learn from you
I cannot be responsible for your indolence.
Now that I am the master, guess who
the real emotional refugee is?

N. Noéll

You Can Have My Seat[31]

As though I've boarded the wrong bus
Watch the flickering roadside brush by
Unfamiliar
We're sitting beside each other
You look at me as though I've forgotten to buy milk with the groceries
A full-knowledge look
I'm unmistakable to you
And you
Are a misty specter popped out of an unearthed ancient
    grave
History
Someone else's history

       I can leave
              I've always been able to leave
I get off
Somewhere
You watch me with a *he-won't-go-far* look
Every step seems *far*
But as *far* gets closer
I realize
It's not that *far* after-all

Keith Nunes

Being in Barcelona, Catalonia, Spain[32]

Feel the spring of energy bubbling from the red earth, alchemy
transforming plants and stones into built forms.

A white-haired woman watches the golden, soaring
altar-screen, a magic thicket, theatre of worship.

Did a gilded leaf just move?

Herod's soldier, framed by paint, grasps the child,
his mama glares through Catalan eyes.

Barcelona—shall we stroll along Las Ramblas, to see Gaudí's
Casa Battló—a molten chocolate arabesque of stone.
See Güell Palace in dark and rigid splendour.

'This cannot be our home', says Senora Gaudí. 'We must move
now, now! And where are the children?'
They are on the roof. 'Oh Mama, see what has sprouted here.'

Gaudí's ghost soulfully prowls between the pinnacles of the
unfinished cathedral…. 'When will this ever end,
    this eternal project of mine?
Where is God's hand to help me? Aaah, he is here….look up at
my celestial cathedral ceiling.'

Joy in rebellion
Such inventiveness knows no
Boundaries. Bravo

Patience O'Neill

Escape
Overture

Black leaves, grey canals, muddled memories,
A slope extending into darkness,
Shimmering stars, murmuring crows, crumbled faces...
You came, you left.

The rose petals you put into the envelope
Along with the morning dew
Still stay in my drawer.

The song I played along with
—*C'est la vie*.
C'est la vie, c'est la vie...

If, if only, you grabbed my hand that foggy night;
If, if only, you kissed my lips under the London plane...

Water reeds, backyards, the blue moon,
Wine bottles, bridge, wuthering trains...
I came, I left.

Jun Pan

Escape
Nocturne

Over 12,000 days,
Bliss, ecstasy, bewilderment, all human emotions
Filled in your life,

A life, started with a letter
With beautifully written calligraphy,
Which, intruding into your girl's dream,
Broke your homely peace.

Softness turned into tenacity;
A girl to a woman.
You fled, you fought, you followed your heart.

The train that did not depart
Carried away your girl's timidity,
Gave away your first nudity
Entirely.

That man
Became part of your life, your body
Bred into, a new life, a new body.

Since then
You left all walls
Behind.

Jun Pan

Escape
Pastorale

Carried in a basket
You escaped hunger,
Brought into a house
Of walls, fields, dramas,
And a husband,
Deprived of love
And literacy.

The tattoo carved into your wrist
Became the only word you recognize,
The only window
To the outside world
That you fear, dread,
Yet eager to embrace
One day...
One day, only one day.

But
The shelter gradually built up
Collapsed
Eventually.

Tree, rope, life taken;
Tears, bombs, fears tighten.

Four new lives,
Four after four,
Home became the second tattoo,
This time, carved into your heart.

You fell in love,
Being loved,
Only to be embraced by darkness
Again.

Rope, door, black moon;
Anguish, pain, broken noon.

You picked up life,
Embraced love.
The two tattoos
Finally found tranquillity
In the river of time,
Integrated into one
Named *Destiny*.

Jun Pan

Escape
Cadence

I dozed off on my desk, you saw me;
I whispered into a boy's ear, you spotted me;
I did not raise my hands high enough doing gym, you yelled
    at me.

Kindergarten, primary, high school—university;
10, 8, 5 minutes—24 hours.
It has to be, it has to be...

I feared, struggled, grew;
Drowning in love
Is a luxury
That takes time to brew.
I didn't know, I didn't know...

Bamboo shoots, jungles, wisteria flowers—
A world to show;
Rivers, seas, oceans—
A map in the row.

Tears, roof top,
That misty night
An invisible rope
Tied to the knight on a horse—

I surrendered.

I surrendered.

A journey to flee
In desire of wings to fly
Or, just imaginary ones,
Which led to
Stop, after stop, after stop...

I flop, flop, and flop,
Falling back
Into your love loop.

Jun Pan

Advancing Dementia

Do I know you?

You seem to think I do.
Almost, I can see
Something familiar in your smile and voice.

I am quite sure I know you
And it's clear that you know me
But even that is difficult…
Sometimes I'm not just me.

I think that I used to know you
In a life not long ago,
When time was something I understood
And I remembered the home where I lived.

You are my mother, my sister,
At other times my daughter.
How can you expect me to know you
When you will not stay the same?
…Changing, always changing.

But now today is a good day,
I see you plain as plain can be.
My heart beats with excitement,
But wait, the clouds move in
…You are gone.

Was it yesterday?
Was it today?
Cold fear blows in with the stranger
She or he I do not know.

Where have you put my daughter?
Have pity, put her back!
I do not wish to know **you!**
Do I know you?

Susan Phillips

Not Forgotten[33]

They don't let the flowers be with her
for their beauty not deserving hers
which dazzles the clouds,
puzzles the haze,
and dwindles the head of castles
into a beast who clings on guarding
the garland and its Aegean owner
from any earthly touches
not to mention the heavenly dust

They don't let the guards leave hold of her
for her want to rule threatening theirs
which glorifies their legacy,
purifies their aristocracy
and beautifies their conspiracy
from a desire which keeps on sealing
the bygones into the envelopes
from any human predicament

They don't let their hearts reach out to her
for her determination insulting theirs
that justifies their bullets,
glorifies their manhood,
and
disguises their fears
which goes on crumbling
the constructs into the wind
blowing
through the sandstorm of hijabs

We might have lost our Lucy
But our Joan is still on the arc.

Danny Dylan Poon

Amber[34]

Still on deck with a few people...
The last boats have left. We are sinking...
Some men are praying. The end is near...

Searching for the oldest messages in bottles,
even after 132 years in ginger ale, holy water,
she is eavesdropping centuries of love, luck, friendships,
pursuing his favorite beer can,
guy ropes of his beach tent.
She once drank the moon with him
champagne upon champagne, thrown to brine.
That perfection so true, it had to end.

Head bowed, she chances upon false eyelashes,
bottle openers, wave-smoothened pebbles,
wreckage to the weight of sand, shore stones.
And walking near Hamburg pockets a stone
that, upon drying, ignites into her coat
setting ablaze memories off postcards.

Passers-by, firefighters come to extinguish
phosphorus from a WW2 incendiary apparatus,
unstable after 65 years—missing chunk,
decaying like pain into her breath, gasps of air,
tremors: 4.5 on a Richter's scale,
entering soil, groundwater—a man-made volcano,
too cold for revenge, too old for regret.

As when he left her like evacuating hundreds
in a child's play of *fire, fire on the mountain,*
in the sky, upon the earth, upon the whole, whole freaking-
fucking-frigging globe.

Rochelle Potkar

Hair By Hair[35]

You want something new. A man,
a woman, a child. Mainly the latter. The sea
will roll in waves of ecstasy, you reveal
the continents, their defenceless shapes.
You don't go to the movies, but your film finishes
at ten past five. Ten past five, they say.
Having Time would be great, were it real:
Our imaginary friend. We caught him in the corner,
as he forced his fists down his own throat!
I came alive with a sharp sense
of compassion, let's go, let's go away, now.
At the bottom, by which I mean at the very bottom,
we found snowballs, scrunched up papers,
and little fishy skeletons. Their fragility stunned me.
Pull it by its hair, with long gazes, say it out loud:
    fences are hedgerows,
their ends are split, the end of dreams,
and you have skin, oh my Goodness, what a skin you have!

Simona Rackova
Translated by Natalie Nera

Dreams Of Evening[36]

Now it is morning.
    I wish it were night.
    I wish I could roll up like a caterpillar
        to hibernate and transform.
    Then after many dawns
        my wings would grow
        stretched by capillaries
        of fresh blood.
Now it is morning.
        Outside, children play at school break.
        Then they become constrained.
    When they go home they will savour
        fried rice and bitter melon gourd.
Evening will roll a veil.
        At night, we will all dream separate dreams
            until the alarm time
                    of awakening.

Joanna Radwańska-Williams
9 November 2015

The Tartness Of Unknowing[37]
For John He

The feeling of not knowing does not vanish.
It is the torture of the open-minded.
It is the sight of time unrolling
        escaping understanding,
the tantalizing smell of the unknown.
Dig deeper, you say, or—
        Catch that fish!
        Too late.
        It has disappeared.
    Sometimes, you dig and dig
    into the wellsprings of the mind
    finding things there
    that you did not put there.
    They have been there since the beginning of the universe.
Sometimes, it is an old book, a find,
      like the tome of Techmer's *Zeitschrift*
retrieved from archival storage
in Chapel Hill library
that had been ordered by a nineteenth-century librarian
    and gathered generations of untouched dust.
There is so much to know, so little time,
That with time the feeling deepens.
Like climbing a mountain,
    the wider the vista's scope below,
    the more unreachable.
The only comfort comes
        from the well inside my mind.

Joanna Radwańska-Williams
10 April 2014

Buttons[38]

Look, the Teflon women approach on high heels
with the Teflon men at their sides,
in their columns of regiments on the May Day boulevard.

They press buttons and sculpt their flesh
and, at night, pull their investment homes around them
like a cocoon of steel.

The desert preacher comes once a week
to water their gardens.
He drives away crazy grass
from their magazine green lawns,
but, in the night, with his followers,
he hunts stars across the dome of the sky,
sitting in a circle in the cooling wastes
outside the irrigation zone.

His daughter, wearing a Big Bang,
is a button in the Biblical desert
waiting to be pushed.

Patrick Reardon

Listening To Chang'e Read
On Mid-Autumn Moon Festival[39]

      Putting the lid on Yang,
      coming home to one's self

Moon-refuged from ten-thousand griefs, Chang'e bids
cello-voiced good-byes to past star-lives, blind
choices, words. *Oh give me myself!* She prays,

scatters ten-thousand cinnamon sticks and reads
her fortune: *Morning, a garden, a pear tree
shading teacher and child reading.*

Lap-propped book invites being both
beneath pear tree and lost in the forest
of characters—this time Narnia's

winter-pages turning right to left flying
them forward—into tyranny's past?
Or blindly backward into the future?

Winged-pages die with each exhale; each pause births
flight-waves—new life's resurgence—the butterfly-way
to surmount tyranny's deception, revealing

the child, Hime's Big Dream: *living is a form
of not being sure, not knowing what, next or how.*
Chang'e regrets she had known the story

but not its mystery: *the moment you know
you begin to die a little.* She inhales
each leap after leap in the dark of pear-wood—

loving, when book covers meet, their infinite kiss.

Melissa Ann Reed

Mid-Autumn Moon Festival,
Lake Harriet, Linden Hills[40]

Lake Harriet Lindens niche us among
fanning almond leaves curling like spindle—
spooned honey lacing apricot tea.

Watermelon sunset flames—*komorabes**
among olive and Chinese red foliage.
Gull wing-blades, like white lily pads, flash silver light.

Is this the day you be waitin' for?
My heart, a geode breaking open like
Lake Harriet, holds the brotherly

African-American's voice in liquid sun.
Waves break into white iris. The sun, now
a tiny golden ball (like the one lost

by fairytale's princess) disappears—drops
to rise on the other side of midnight.
An empty rowboat drifts, trailing the moon—

a ripe peach testing ebony boughs.
Night's cobalt entrance chiaroscuros the moon's
jellyfish fingers meeting phosphorescing grass.

Woodland birds crack seeds that snap like wood-burning logs.
Grown gravid, the silver yin moon, astride
Linden s-curves, pours ambrosia to fill the world.

She is I; she is you, lacking nothing.

Melissa Ann Reed

*Komorabe *is Japanese for 'a curtain of sunshine shimmering through foliage'.*

White Clouds, Red Trees[41]
for Angelina

White clouds sail through Beijing branches,
pressing heavy limbs from trunks that float
on thin mountain air. Lan Ying launches
his scroll in quick water. Silked colours coat
red the leaves set adrift. It is autumn—
dew soon to spread jade white stairs over grass,
gold cicadas soon to drone the ripening of plums,
earth soon to wrap new seed in warm humus,
harvested grains soon to leave brown vistas—
camouflage of migrant pheasants. Burning
yellow *c*hrysanthemums will announce Ninth
Moon Festival and winter's deepening dream.
Earth's deep gratitude for life bows down.
The world is hollow and profound.*

Melissa Ann Reed

**Zhuangzi's phrase as he likened the depth of autumn to a man standing on a mountain, seeing the truth of the world with greater clarity.*

Signals[42]

Trapped …
        like a mime in a box
I push against boundaries I cannot see.
My struggles for Freedom
—efforts in Futility.

I plead, I shout,
Banging on the confines of this
               —body.
I am inside
and *I—want—to—get—out*.

~ ~ ~
   Stillness,
        Quiet,
               WhiteLight
                    ~ ~ ~

A crackle, A spark,
        The start of a New day;
Synapses firing,
        Signals finding their Way—

A toe moves, a fingertip twitches,
        all odds it Defies;
A deep breath of Longing, and
… *I open my eyes.*

Vinni Relwani

Homo Erectus[43]

Pungent cold
sharp as a February
night without commas
without punctuation
the rare passers do not speak
they have frozen words and hands.
Events curve me
only a trill of trumpet
to warm my soul
an idea
to pursue the next day
to the reconquest
of the erected position.

Angelo Rizzi

I Count The Inert Hours

It is an uncaring night
to words
indifferent to the gripping sleep
that haunts me
at the first autumn cold
indifferent to everyone
because nobody passes.
It is a voiceless night
which leaves space to expression
to vocation
to a deep sigh.
I count the inert hours
passing too slowly
a monotonous, boring night
like an abyss
but I feel the sense
patience teaches me.
Ungraspable night
the rhythm beyond me
timeless night
where thoughts are placed
in the hourglass of life.

Angelo Rizzi

The Notebook

I can not find
the notebook where I write
it may be under a book
inside a pocket
under a sky of white pepper
inside a roar of ideas.
I have to write
of ginger moons
naming months
and of my friend trees.
I have to tell
of friendly voices
of the dripping hours
slipping away
swallowing each other.
I have to write
of fragments of life
of grim events
of the current impatient condition
then active
in an eternal movement.

Angelo Rizzi

Driving My Lips To The Rainclouds[44]

Ears absorb the chaos
I have kissed you on your ears
Thighs are the raging bulls
        up against the ground
I have kissed you on your thighs
I have kissed you up to skies
It roared

I have kissed you on your face

It rained
I have kissed you on your tears
         on your fears
I have kissed you on your smell
I have kissed you on your meteors

What once covered my lips now discovered
         Earth
             in you

Halil Suat Saraç

Schoolyard Memories[45]

Beneath the scarlet oak
nearby the parking lot
we came in throngs to cloak
our breathing that was shot
through and through with hopes
of an early end.

No one wanted to confess
as the one controlled by fear,
so we cast lots to choose the stranglers
and soon the chosen ones appeared.
They used to be our peers
but, reabsorbed by Nature,
became
the prosthesis of that crippled Fall.
—have I made myself quite clear?—;
their duty was to strangle *all*.

Once it was I, I still recall
how life did writhe
beneath my palms
it said, "I am not it,
I am not life, so let me go..."
But the throat wriggled in a
melody of throes.

More often still I offered it—
this diaphanous pillar,
through which trickle air and blood
in torrents
to connect my heart and brain,
in that gesture which they call
a consciousness,
and I, a cosmic pain.

And there we stood aligned,
gathered like apostles
beneath the autumn sky
that none called prematurely
the azure of his lover's eye.

I wanted for the strangler
to encompass my neck
and sow on the fallow lands of thought
a crop of dreams and death.

They strangled till I fell
on the bed of leaves…
The diadem of dirt
that crowned me as I lay
in suffocated mirth
among signs of fit decay
I didn't wear for long.

They strangled till I fell
alone on the edge of night—
a night of short duration
for soon I heard that dampened sound
of my lids as they unlocked again
and the autumn sky unfurled
the blue of its own large lid
forever closed in consternation.

Sanja Särman

The Burier Of Flowers Lamenting

"The blossoming flowers are easy to see, the fallen ones hard to seek
At the threshold sorrow kills the burier of flowers.
(花开易见落难寻, 阶前愁杀葬花人)"—Cao Xueqin

(The first two stanzas set to the melody of *Angelus ad virginem.*)

Willow catkins fill the air, a spray of thready crystal.
To entomb such fickle corpses, you need to be a vestal,
a virgin who will fade like them, like the falling petals
that sink in muddy waters, never to rise again…

You will commemorate this spring and be its slave
forever, and mourn its blossoms as they fall
aligned like soldiers marching
on this battleground of tepid blasts in March…

Buds burdened by efflorescence…
Beauty broke the back of youth;
and where it fell without a sound
no monument was raised.
We trample underfoot the fallen clusters.
We grind their tissue down to dust.
They melt in dirty downwards flowing streams,
thin flakes of ethereal colors…

At the threshold,
hesitating to dig
a shallow tomb
for this heartless waste
which is spring,
she staggers
and leans on the rake
beneath which flowers sprawl
in their promiscuous death.

Sanja Särman

The Fog

"All's vast that vastness means"—Francis Thompson

All's vast that towards vastness leans.
Crown jewels wrought from sickly queens.
All's vast that vastness means
    —and so this fog, a feather god has shed,
a thready milk of humid smog, terraces that hold
an audience of dead.
In this galaxy of mist, of vaporized dust,
there is no fear of death, and no demented lust.
All's vast that vastness seems:
the moistened masks of men
emerging from this defiled down
to sink back therein again,
into the paling abyss of this beleaguered town.
The mist—a temporary wall,
a downwind fleeting prison
of liquefied white jade.
It has the bluish hue
that once
on your cheeks
belied the vertigo in you.
For you—you always feared
a greatness drawing near
that would interfere with all you said and did
and reduce you to the tremble that your century forbids.
But all's vast that vastness sees
and some, like you, were born to freeze
before the vision of the vast
fog that throws a trembling bridge
between the present and the past.

Sanja Särman

The Only Thing
for Yukio

The only thing worse than a blinded Ajax
is an Ajax maddened by sight.
The only thing worse than a god-sent madness
is madness feigned for a rite.
The only thing more red than murder
is the theatre of pity—his heart—
that was swayed by an infinite softness
that bore both his blood-thirst and art…
The only tear hotter than treason
is a pretended threat—
To shout, "Kneel!" to the world as you hang yourself
before, in its side of indifferent rock,
you twist your blade of paper and lace…
To shout, "Bleed!" to the sea as you drain yourself
in its gently rolling embrace…

The only thing worse than sparing your victims
out of a mistake divine
is to make your countrymen lovers and allies
before whom you can incline
in that last celestial bow,
in which all your entrails at last lie prostrate…

The only thing more belated
than insight into one's crime
is a man who *never once* hated
his defeated country, or time.

Sanja Särman

The Talking Photo

Aunty Trinidad tells,
that soon after she arrived in heaven,
an angel that back on Earth had been a little bit a con artist
and a little bit her brother-in-law,
showed up with a trumpet for annunciations
and a blackboard because he couldn't speak.
His voice in this world was prisoner in a very strange
and captive way.

Aunty, who knew the ways of life,
laughed for the first time after her funeral
and fed up of the blackboard, said to him that
only the Sun, the Moon and the vehemence
—that's how she called the pushes of sex—
come back to the world
and that she would believe otherwise only
when the son comes back to the mother's belly
or the statue of Don Juan in Seville comes back to the lost wax.

My voice didn't die, it stayed in a photo, wrote the angel,
and that photo is on Earth, that's why I come to you, Trini,
I've waited so long for you.

And then it all changed.

Aunty Trinidad remembered,
with an unaccustomed shock,
that I had a talking photo. Sometimes talking a lot,
sometimes quiet for weeks.
I have it in the living room,
inside a frame from El Corte Ingles,
in front of the TV and next to a phone (where a vengeance
that is not relevant now was born),
some bottles of smells of the middle class and
my albums with all the family lies.

Very few know about the talking photo—
I never receive visits at home
and Mrs Raquel, who does not fear the dead
but the followers of Mr Trump, cleans it with a bit of bad mood,
quiet or talking—

I have heard that voice, from someone
behind the camera
that took the photograph of my parents
on their wedding day,
hundreds, thousands of times.

My beliefs guide me without excess
and always welcome me
when I look at the watch, stopped at 8.15
in Hiroshima;
or when I take a bath in the waters where the African immigrants sink;
or when the shame of being born in a country of thieves
    burns.

These are my secrets.
The things that accompany me also have secrets:
the switched off TV with the Twin Towers inside,
the phone, the bottles, the albums.

And the photo where a hidden man whispers

    "It's done. Tonight, at nine."

Finally I know whose is the voice of the talking photo.
What I don't know is who listened and why it mattered.
She will never tell me,
Aunty Trinidad.

José Manuel Sevilla

A Grace Of Light[46]

It was on a day when the sun's ray
streamed through the clouds to a blessing place
deep in the woods where my feet did stray
leaving the path with nary a trace
to tell my homefolk that I had been there
bending and climbing to make myself free . . .
to leave behind all my worldly care.
It was on that day grace came for me.

A funnel of light appeared from the sky
and came to rest on an opening of ground
turning this earth to a *holy-on-high*
a pilgrim place where guidance is found.
Kneeling in this light, my soul found release—
troubles still come but this light does not cease.

Allegra Jostad Silberstein

Let This Refuge Sing
(*A villanelle*)[47]

'Twitter, sweet birds, and make my morning sing.
Chirrup away such solemn nightly fears
that in my thoughts, I fly with you on wing.

Bell like, I beg you sweetly warble. Swing
my mournful musings, now brine-washed with tears.
Twitter, sweet birds, and make my morning sing.

Let me thrum your melodies, let me ring
a peal of joy, morphing moments to years,
that in my thoughts, I fly with you on wing.

When shadows cross my mind, 'tis no great thing
to dream some dark, forgotten fancy nears:
twitter, sweet birds, and make my morning sing,

E'er doubt prevails in damning earthly sting,
 transmute my mind to mellifluous cheers
that in my thoughts, I fly with you on wing.

Flutter, larks. Chirp-chirrup-trill past dread, fling
dull dreams to ditches: melancholy clears.
So twitter bright birds, let this refuge sing,
that in my thoughts, we'll fly awhile on wing.

Hayley Ann Solomon

My Refuge For A While[48]

In teardrops laced with rare sunlight,
a rainbow bright stops by;
each curve an arc so sweet a sight
my heightened thoughts ask, "Why?"

Refractions quite enrapture me,
enhanced I am, entranced I be,
with all the shades you've let me see.

I'm fully free to fly.

Your love has altered all I feel,
transformed with reeling heat
the murky greys I shed and peel
as sealed I am from sleet.

Now sunrise colours so infuse
the deepest of my heart's own bruise,
that giddy lights in all their hues
my darkest muse shall greet.

I'm coloured by your sparkling wit,
enraptured by your style
I'm incandescent, wonder-lit:
You flutter-flit your smile,

As dewdrops glisten on my skin,
I can't believe the dream I'm in,
Your every kiss, your quirky grin,

My refuge for a while!

Hayley Ann Solomon

There Never Was Nothing[49]

There never was nothing—
only a long loneliness.
The heavens breathed frost,
blanketing everything in
a darkness too dull to breathe.

For eons, not a sound
and not an echo of a sound, relieved the loneliness.
Then Muri-ranga-whenua, the grandmother,
    looks to the stars.
She sees a canvass of black, dotted with light,
the thousand jewels of the blanket of night.

There's a collision of reds and greens,
white and pearl, pale and bright, flame and flicker,
hotter, colder, farther, nearer than even she—
in her ancient greatness—can conceive.

When she closes her eyes for the long sleep,
the fabric of her mind pieces patterns:

Koru unfurling infinitely slowly,
the drip drip drip of stalactites,
or roots of Rata stealthily reaching the forest floor.
A flash of red—Rata rising to the sky in bold-blossoming
gladness. Pohutakawa blushes. Rimu is forever
caressed to submission, subsumed by Rata.
The forests dance.

They dance with life as the patterns form swiftly—the crash
and curl of water, the carving of mountains with blades of ice,
the rush, the ready rush of water to sea, the curling krill, the
soaking sponges, the fingers of coral that brighten
immense volumes of darkness.

Unimaginable are the pressures, the light of the heavens
and the far depths where no creature lives.

Gravity and antigravity, matter and antimatter, and
the tiny, beautiful moments that matter most.

Murirangawhenua blesses all this as her refuge.

Hayley Ann Solomon

Building Wharf

'I don't knock myself out,' he said.
'Mostly I just tinker.'
He was at it for six months.
The wharf was a monolith—
a construction made of wood and plastic
that jutted out into the water.

My father is an engineer—
the wharf bore the hallmarks of his design.
It floats upon the water—
And will float there after his death,
A memento.

It's something for his grandchildren
to play on
or dive off if they are game enough
into the murky waters
down, down, into the tangled weeds.

It's an entity for the ducks to perch on
squawking to each other
in their own special language
duck-speak, unintelligible
to the human ear.

My father takes pride in the wharf
It's a retirement achievement
A man needs hobbies
To keep himself busy
We all know what happens
To idle hands
Heaven forbid
The devil should take his
At this stage of life.

I made a special trip
to the family farm
to see the wharf
to find inspiration for this poem.

I found what I was looking for.
A poem in the form of a jetty.
Jutting out into the water—
Solid for generations to come.

Laura Solomon

The Party

You have to be dead to be invited to this party.
As is to be expected, all the stars are here.
Janis, Marilyn, Jesus.
There are ordinary people too though.
Kevin Watson who died of a blood clot to the brain
shortly after his 40th birthday.
He's been resurrected. Now he's partying in the corner—
he's put himself in charge of the music
and is playing Nirvana
as Cobain toys with a segment of his blown-off head.
Other run-of-the-mill folk present?
Jimmy Molesworth who hanged himself
and is now hitting on Janis Joplin who is oblivious
to the attention, dancing wildly to *Come As You Are*
a whisky bottle clutched tightly in her right hand.
Jimmy's still got rope marks around his neck.
There's Cindy Rutherford who was hit by a car
while simultaneously cycling and listening to her iPod.
Not a good combination. She's got splinters of glass
from the windscreen embedded in her face.
Marilyn decides to re-stage her death for our general
entertainment.
She strips off and swallows a bottle of pills.
Then passes out in the bed. Nobody looks alarmed.
It's all faked; we can't die now that we're dead.
The black telephone rings.
I move to answer it.
Nobody is there.
I can hear the 22nd Century heavy breathing down the line.

Laura Solomon

In The Waves Of Midnight

I have witnessed my people
migrating through salt & water.

They hurled their sacks of clothes
from the boat to the shore.

From wood to embers, & from ashes
to homes, mothers kept past lives in their pockets.

I have listened to grandma's bedtime stories
turning into a grocery list.

There once was a pastor
who ran away to become a farmer.

He planted cucumbers, lettuce,
milk, & Dutch biscuits...

I have passed down the family fables
to my younger cousins, to my many nephews & nieces.

Here, our ancestors held out their baskets
as they baked their dough under the sun.

Lavender has grown into an adolescent,
a burning flame into a silent daughter.

I have kissed the earth out of loneliness,
dirt, snow & mooncakes taste the same.

I have fallen in love with a stranger on the mountain
knowing I will never see her again.

I have roamed the lands to find my grave.

Here, I have baptized myself shirtless
in the waves of midnight,

as the water fills my mouth,
I can see the ashes rising to life.

Jeddie Sophronius

Dogbite

you know I keep on

circling artificial lakes
like hurricane Dorothy;
and all the little dogs are

snapping at my ankles.
benevolent injectables
diminishing the bite;

I'll wait until I'm rabid.

wrest my shaking legs
into a cataclysmic event.
stop leaving food out for

triceratops-masked lovers;
see, each one's a puppy in
the right nostalgic light.

not saying I miss you too.

and any mask could tell you
extinction equals beauty.
and any dog could tell you

loneliness is violence;
and an infection's just
an invitation, sorry

to be such a pain.

Andrew Sutherland

Five Blessings

the last time I visited home,
I cheated on you five (5) times.

Once for poor luck, like
realising you hadn't studied
hard enough and had to
cheat the exam; sort of a
learning-curve, a jog uphill, health
(1) check-up.

Twice for volume; never go
half-assed, and on the two
(mister nice who came so sweet),
the home hit home and I cried
in strange arms, winner of a wealth
(2) of tears.

the Next, like stasis, vision
obscured until all I saw were
those disappointed ejaculators,
my ancestors; the past crowding
clouding, haranguing me to a long life,
(3) sightless.

Fourth, I fell in love, over
drinks and art-chat, took
him back to second family's
bed and set him down in
sister Sharda's sheets; love and love of virtue,
(4) leaving.

and Last, like nothing at all,
entered me with no more
effort than a DM, a little
taste of nowhere, hardly
aware of every spill. Such a peaceful death,
(5) my home.

Andrew Sutherland

Terminal One

When you left me at
the airport, you named
me as a liar. And my lies
are your armour, I know.
But the very best ones
are promises to God. To-
morrow, I'll be grateful.
Tomorrow, I'll be good.
And tomorrow, so true.

At three a.m. before I woke
you, I packed my bags and
wondered why I kept finding
salt shakers in every room.
Perhaps I'm terrified of
becoming possessed. Keep
the demons out. Ironic
that I was so keen to be
in your possession. Is evil
to feel no guilt or is evil
endless guilt? But in practice
they're the same.

I sleep horribly here.
There's a possum in the ceiling,
apparently. So it's not
the ghosts that got to me,
in the end. Except you—
my jiangshi. I wanted
to name you Possum, but
I've always been sickened
by cute nicknames, and
it's close enough to a lie
for you to reject it.

One day I'll bury you
in a mound made of quilts,
shake the salt in circles
and keep you
forever; never
wrong you again.
(I tried not to lie.)

Andrew Sutherland

Alley Cat Detective

After midnight, I seek the scoundrel
who broke into an elderly man's home,
shot him point blank in his bed.

I sense the perp's nearness,
sneak into an alley,
spot him against a dumpster,
approach from behind,
yowl, nip his ankles,
as a police car appears.

The startled suspect is apprehended.
After shoving the handcuffed crook into the back of the patrol car,
an officer turns, bends, strokes me.
I purr, rub against his ankle,
then slink away, my night's work done.

Abigail Taylor

Abandoned Beauty[50]

The doll looks hopeful
on her custom-made chair
in her frills covered with dust.
She is still waiting to resume a life that
honoured her until not long ago.

The child who loved her so much
is a girl now
playing tennis outdoors
coming to her room
for her homework, or just to sleep.

The beautiful doll blends in the
roomscape, among heaps of books
and clothes, and rackets.

The doll's hair is graying with dust,
her dress's colour is fading too.
Only the eyes continue to look,
to stare at the wall,
with their happy angles still cheerful
in the long, impossible wait

Luisa Ternau

For So Sweet Is The Sound Of My Lute[51]

With an icy look
she dismissed me stating,
"Most people are in need of society
some by society are needed;
I was poor too
but I understood the formula
and worked my way
to be needed—greatly.
Cover your
wound!", she yelled,
"You obviously made it yourself.
It moves no one
to pity!"

Thus in my youth
I was harangued
by a passing courtesan
while begging
by the main gate
for me
and my siblings.

Now I wander from castle
to city. From city to castle.
I play my lute
in beautiful halls,
where rich tapestries
hang from the wall,
mostly obtained by the
killing of many. People
that in life may
have been needed
or not. Certainly,
their lot was to die
in a battle not fully understood
and be swallowed
into rapid forgetfulness.

I do not sport a self-inflicted wound now,
I do not need to elicit pity to get more coins.
But in my sojourning abroad,
every-one runs to hear my lute.
Thus I lost the shack I called home,
where my siblings were waiting for me.
In the notes of my lute
I can only but dream of it.

Just the hope to play in Heaven
after all this wandering
makes me go from castle to city
from city to castle and beyond.

Along the path I may stop
and play my lute to the trees,
while I watch the sound
reaching for the
sun.

Luisa Ternau

Seller Of Dreams[52]

One morning
I crossed the border
Into a foreign land
A man from the mall came to me
Asking me to follow him
To his shop
"What do you sell?"
"Dreams"
"No, thanks"
I moved on
But he kept mumbling
Close to me
"Go away!" I urged him

Returning later to the border
I saw him again
He looked at me
—If he recognised me
I do not know—
He was still inviting
Passers-by to his shop
"Have you sold any dream today?"
"Nobody buys my stuff"
I was moved
And followed him to his shop

Layers and layers
Of ordinary things everywhere
—"Where are the dreams?"

Dreams are here
As they are everywhere
Just open your eyes
They come to you
Without you knowing

Dreams
Will dissolve like ghosts

Dreams
Will be there
At the hour of death

Dreams
Will change your life

They will not run away
From you
Like me
Chasing you
Until the end of time

Luisa Ternau

Tuscan Autumn[53]

Hiking
the rock and packed dust
trails in
the Tuscan hills,
it hasn't rained
for months,
a guide proclaims,
"Not a tear of rain."

Through brown-leafed vineyards
and tilled fields,
past parched olive trees
with skeletal branches,
farm houses with
fragile field stone walls
and sun-faded tiled roofs;
in the distance
ancient churches bake
in the last of
summer's heat.

I was startled
by ghosts
their stories filled
the hot morning air
I breathed,
as faint images
appeared
near me.

Their ancient witness
testified to many
dry seasons
and to lives,
centuries ago.

"We've worked and drunk and
loved here,"
they murmured

as sweat darkened my back;
their voices
lost long ago
but only to those
not listening.

What
caused me
to listen?
I did not
intend to, but
was enchanted
by their tales,
amazed
that the long-dead
could be so
alive.

Edward Tiesse

The Failure Of Typhoons[54]

As the months move on, and June turns into July,
The typhoons come and go and the rain pours from the sky.
The streets are full of water and the trees bend like begging monks
As the wind turns into fury and keeps people at home in their bunks.
The restaurants all are closed and there's nowhere we can dine,
The shops are shut and we can only eat sandwiches with wine.

The planes that normally land on a regular local runway
Are all diverted to distant islands where the wind is a gentle sway
And the passengers spend the night in small hotels and bars
Until the typhoon lets peace return to earth and brings out all the stars.
The air is peaceful once again and the streets are clean and dry
As life returns to normal from the sea up to the sky.

But, though the typhoon's passing lets peace come back to town,
A flood of political egos spreads chaos from the top down.
No matter where they come from—East, West, North or South—
They love to have a loud and noisy mouth,
For their behaviour is controlled by a single drive—
The passionate desire to ensure their fame and power thrive.

They play endless games, denouncing innocent citizens,
Claiming they are defending the state against some dangerous netizens,
And never admit that the daily news is fake and just designed to give
Them the self-admiration they need to live.
They hate meditation and literature, and ignore Dickinson's warning
Not to shout like a frog in front of an admiring bog every morning.

If only the typhoons could blow these ambitious clowns
Into the sea or sky, we would always have smiles and not
frowns,
But so far the typhoons have failed to make the world a
peaceful place;
And Presidents and Prime Ministers still desire to win some
political race.

So maybe typhoons should blow along every global road,
And wash the streets and alleys and give humanity an ego-free
abode.

Roger Uren

Stain[55]

Honesty
that startling stain,

like semen on a shirt,

or a hump of hide
on the road,

like ink on a page,

or a cheerleader's spotting
in front of a crowd.

A map of honesty
upon your face
like vitiligo.

At our walnut table
ringed
with water spots,

you tell me how
our marriage meant
nothing to you.

To our children,
and our neighbours
and my parents:

I am left
to explain the stain.

Peter Verbica

Magic Hell[56]

Put the cigarettes in a drawer
That way you don't smoke too much
Drop the lighter on the floor
Outside the bathroom
To prevent withdrawals
Don't buy new spoons

In 2006 I visited a needle-exchange van
Run by a sociology professor
Who was once addicted, now reduces harm
I took pictures and interviewed people
Part of a project
After Frank Czernek's death
A project about fentanyl

Chinese producers pump patches
Into the populace
Immoral, amoral? Local dealers
Flood the streets with highs

What is it like to be high?
It is not caring for a moment
A different consciousness
Though my experience is limited
To green puffs and hits

Why do we harm ourselves?
To be someone else
To not sit with ourselves
We cannot stand the bulge
Or the urge to indulge

How can we seek refuge?
Social breakdown is the cause
Depression, loneliness at large
In the society
Problems with money
And self-worth

How can it be repaired?
Give the hopeless hope
Give the people jobs
Don't look down upon
Someone misunderstood

In all the craving
We all feel
Some are under the heel
Of more powerful biological pulls

In all the craving
We all feel
We can never feel full

From plants, we make a magic hell
Where is the respite?

David Vognar

Poems[57]

I.
There was once a blind horse in a mine shaft,
and a canary was his only friend.

When stumbling through the shafts, the horse would say
to the canary: oh, bro', you're far away
you have a better life, don't ask me why…

The canary just cheerfully agreed
and sang with all his might: that's all I need,
I only came here so that I can die

II.
Blind going deaf—if happens this
go cold all over apple trees.
That trembling sent of fear.
And iron racks
torture the tongue up there.

III.
Miracle
It is expected
It will come, for sure.
Maybe
it chooses that man
Maybe
It will happen to this woman
Splat, splat, steps of the barefoot whores
Let go of me, you gloomy darkness

Olga Walló

Cross

It starts with a kiss
A bomb
Dropping into the sea
Several rounds of waves

The kiss
Turned into miss
And miss to chase
Around the campus
For just one path

The bed
Welcomes the longing

Small it is
Big it is

The game
The death
The breath
The game
The dream

Over the north
Over the south

Cross

Anson Wang

My Jellyend

A purple umbrella, you came
A flickering ripple, I saw
Yellow, brown, circles, we met

Anson Wang

Ride With A Spider

88R
Central to City One
In the middle of the afternoon

Nobody

Went to the upper deck for my favourite seat
The very front row facing the big window
Feeling like sitting on a roller coaster

Several stops
Nobody

A spider
The size of a lotus seed
Strolling around the top

A little frightened
I thought of moving
Leaving the full view to the spider

Watching closely
And reluctant to move

The spider kept its manners
Just striding backward and forward on the top
With no intention of invading

What a relief
I garrisoned my castle
Enjoying the heat from the occasional sun

More stops
Nobody

The spider
And me

City One

Anson Wang

The Little One And The Sea

The little one wakes up at four
Before the sun knocks at the door

He gazes through the windows
Standing on his toes

Birds singing happily outside
He listens attentively inside

The sea blinks with a yawn
Leaning back on the mountains

Still is the sea
And the little one

Anson Wang

It Was April Fool's Day
In Memory Of Leslie Cheung Kwok-wing

The eve before April Fool's day
We walked across the bridge to the Star Ferry Pier.
It was a night of full-moon,
And warm summer breeze.
Our genial faces looked gentle and tender under the moonlight.

April Fool's day is hot and dry.
In the afternoon I take the bus to the airport.
On the upper floor
Children are clamouring like cicadas,
Their harsh summer decibels resounding through my body,
from eardrums to toes.
An ice cream might comfort my restless heart.
I recall the vanilla ice cream in the hand of that little boy by the
Star Ferry last night.

Last night, I took the Star Ferry from TST to Central.
Scattered by the sea breeze, my petal tears
Brushed the last shades of spring from my eyelashes and hair.
All that luminous architecture near and far
Threw glistening pink and purple lights into the calm darkness,
Left the white moonlight contemplating the silence from on
high.

If that day had also been a day with full moon,
Would you still have chosen that lone journey?

I climbed the stairs at the Fringe Club,
Thoughts rambling through my mind:
'Leslie was standing here',
'On the upper step, just here.'
Then,
my face contorted,
And I knew from the soles of my feet
I'd lost the last trace of warmth.

The bus is speeding across the Tsing Ma Bridge.
On the upper floor of the airport bus,
Children finally feel fatigued and sleep like little angels.
The warmth of the sunlight soaks into my skin,
Gradually
We all become slower than the time passing.

Today is April Fool's day,
Someone is kayaking slowly upstream.
Someone is hiking among mountain briars.
Someone has departed,
Someone has arrived.
A fly buzzes on the window-pane,
Trying to conquer its sense of weight loss
From the speeding bus.

It was April Fool's day,
You fooled us and then you went
Away.

Giovena Wang Songwenjia

8 Months In Warsaw, 1939[58]

July: It is scalding summer in the pond / at the park, reprieve for the blush / of skin exposed too soon as / we splash the water barely hearing / any news, the threats from the border / like clouds circling, the government / says *no cause for worry*, yet they / thick-spread gas masks like buttered bread, / to be prepared, they said, though *cavalry / will stop our goose-stepping neighbours*. *August:* The call-up letter & father / packs bags to beat a path to the / train, just that fast, his feinting waves / to Rachel & Mother, me & Brother, / our lives left to live unchanged, as lovely as always & he will write from Palestine / & return, lacking thought / that later might mean never. *September:* The first day of bombings & we watch / the distance blow like whales' plumes, / our pilots' guns puncture like balloons, / the plummeting & blaze & cratering over there, all that smoke / a refinery blacking air, but theatres & shows / & dinners that night say nothing ever / happened, & everything filled to capacity. *October:* Just one month later, our street / is pocked by tank shots, the house next door / piles of brick & beams & grumbling over rubble, & we are blasted / more, & spend weeks with no water, digging- / out, Warszawa nights displaying flames / instead of sparkling autumn stars, we watch / skies explode in various shades of wreck. *November:* & fabric stars to separate neighbours / from neighbours & a wall bricking-up with the fear of typhus greeting/ half a million souls, & new laws, even one for basic bread: 2 ounces growing green / mold & rummage through garbage each day / the gold: potato peels & what have you, / & long lines for the lack of everything else / you could ever want. *December:* Now there are twenty in our flat, / three taken in the black night for beating, / more spaces on the floor, more room for me / in dreams of waving fields, the grain of Otwock / just last year, long before I wake to shivers / & remember Warszawa in winter. *January:* If G-d could have eyes—I imagine / rabbis say—if G-d could have / ears, I wonder, could he stand / the shrieks of the beggar boy bashed / in his blood, frozen at the border / that they bricked & barbed, on New Year's Day? *February:* There is something beyond the bones / that stretch skin's uneven humps, / there is something beyond the thrust / of nausea for dinner, beyond water / I pass that pretends it's solid; / if I were to think, I seem to have lost / the taste of every dream & I have to ask: If I had one day left, how then, would I live it?

Bruce Wasserman

Snake In Hiding By St Peters Billabong

The tail curls beside the path half worn by odd passers-by.
The head faces the water that's heavy, oily in mid-summer
    heat,
surface scribbled by striders and swallows after them.

The snake's scopic body lies in three languid waves
that could have been copied from a child's drawing,
tongue poking out between compressed lips.

It used to be fragments of fine china, bright clay pots,
and many-hued shards of glass:
given new life by a careful alchemist

of no name who set each little piece here in the good earth
under the gurgle of magpies by day and the buzz of sunsets'
    cicadas.
Though kaleidoscopic she's easy to miss,

snug under patches of sand and tufting scrub.
Brush and cut and there she is, safe in the ochre earth.
Bright-eyed, venom-free, she waits, and will wait for waking
time

when her dry tongue will flicker will moisten, and lead her
    bejewelled body
to the water that also waits, the water that sings with voices
of the many who came to drink, too many to count

George Watt

Trying Too Hard

Like a singer
without flaw
(though end Ts just too curt)

Sometimes

like a meadow
rendered without blemish

I

the grave pianist
too loud too soft
too studied

fear

like an old fashioned
eye-rolling Hamlet

trying too hard

always then something sweet, vulnerable
vanishes.
Musick's mask slips
and the Muses sigh.

George Watt

Why?

It starts as you arrive.
For the clip-clop of well-shod feet on wet cobbles,
your breathless coming, little eyelets of water
sparkling on your coat—breath misty at the door.
Your case tucked under your coat to keep out rain.

For its affable placement on the table—your
pale hand moving along its black length,
a caress you didn't want others to see. For tension

springing in two opening clicks,
revealing a myriad of keys each a mirror for
our shy faces in a cockeyed room.

For your knee bent as you play,
just so, at the end of a tense thigh,
that thick muscled conduit from head to foot, foot to heart.

Finally, for the Pandora's box of sounds you produced—
sometimes a feather on a thermal wave: then a kite in a
    storm,
a fat duck fighting to fly, or a high eagle's eye:
all more than enough to urge a saint from the grave,
or an operatic howl from the most affectionate of dogs.

Why? That's why.

George Watt

Obliquy[59]

is all
lime brilliant-heated
a stage climb
trestle, balcony
perched one moment
feathery steps to the bower
she inhabits.

uncomforted actor
pressing action
the not him
on others.

some persona chirps
vocal music
scarce uttered then echoed
in everyone's mind
but his own.

the quickened heart
stirs in oblique ways,
takes flight, lifts, wings and swoops,
greeting the perfect stranger to itself
who loves.

Richard Westley

She Believes[60]

She is like many other refugees,
Broken reeds of painful rejection.
Talking to her God, she flees
From despair and destruction.
She believes she too can win
And enjoy life like other people.
With strength of character she'd pin
Hope on dignity: at times quite feeble,
Never taking things for granted,
She believes she is not a lounger,
Upon her prayers she has counted
She believes she is not a scrounger
She believes, too, that strangers smile—
For her they'd even walk an extra mile.

Elizabeth (Libby) Wong

Fairy Tales

In tales they bar the door from the enemy.
We keep our hearts close-guarded,
Surprised to find it ain't like the book.
Family and marriage.

"How much time passes?" you said.
"Find the answers," says the puzzle man.

If you touch a petal of the pale pink rose,
Now, when whored and hoar-frosted,
(Something that's shown plain in the glass)
I see that with you,
It had come again.

The dress and crown on,
The brother Prince,
The procession and train.
Lucky, this time I had put an arm out.
Sniffed at and grasped at—
And found a way,
to something precious.

I have coffers full of gold:
Blood flows again.
Laugh, sing up a perfect storm.
Swing light around; dolls dance and delight.
I rest. There reigns a queen,
With the flowers in her hair
and song at her lips.

Cindy Wyles

Vanity Fair[61]

The ground mightn't shake,
But it's on the stroke of twelve
When I spot her, standing there.
I could not help but stare:
a twin, a duplicate, or fake.

Bleached blond hair;
Too much tan,
Run to fat;
Well then, that's the end of that:
as if I care!

It's a blow to authenticity.
I share a stage.
Struck dumb, I wonder
How on Earth can there be
her there, and here me?

How many more of us exist?
Where is God in this?
Hansel and Gretel, Jekyll and Hyde.
How I felt was, as the monster
that wasn't Adam, for Frankenstein.

Pennies pushed over the edge of the shelf,
Cotton-candy smiles; coconut shies,
Air-gun sound, and identical targets fall to the ground:
I look around: if she's in the crowd, am I more or less lonely?
Bull's-eye and I am more myself.

Cindy Wyles

Dragon's Breath / Inspiration[62]

Crimson
vehement
red
passion feels
like a dragon's exhale
on your skin
and
when it hits
in parallel lines
below your brows
you light up like a match
and burn
burn
burn

and that's when the mystical
starts
hands take control
neurons breaking
synapses connecting
clicking
collapsing
electrical inspiration
whether it be
with a pen
or brush
or C majors
you tailor
your own little
reality
encapsulated
with your essence
a fountain fuelled
by the immeasurable
past future,
space time
the giant climb
before you.

This newborn
baby
born into
creation,
born out of your
hands,
born along
the arborescent
wrinkles
ridges of your fingertips
and time.

Look closer and
you'll mirror
reflections
of yourself
staring
back.

Anthea Yip

To My Love, In A Mysterious Universe

Nothing created
And nothing destroyed—
Just infinite cycles of Dark Matters.
Oh but then!

One volcanic dawn
The innovative
Atoms built you out of carbon and string.

You, of atmosphere
Born, fell to earth where
Relativity reigns absolutely.

Chronicler of storms,
Eating rice and stars,
You lived alone while time arced overhead.

At last, neighbours met—
I found you chasing
Pages from a book the wind had shaken loose.

We caught one chapter,
The rest blew away.
Your strange diary—gossip for sparrows.

But that sole chapter
I lose nights reading.
Candle, is this a man or a riddle?

On sore eyes I press
Cool chrysanthemums.
In this darkness, only now do I see.

Eureka.

Nothing created
And nothing destroyed.
But you ache to know what it means to be.

Sally Younger

THE POETS
brief biographies provided by the poets

Author of three books of poetry, VINITA AGRAWAL is a Mumbai based, award winning poet and writer. She is Editor of Womaninc, a platform for Gender issues. Recipient of the Gayatri GaMarsh Memorial Award for Literary Excellence, USA, 2015, Vinita's poems have appeared in international journals, including *Asian cha*, *Pea River Journal*, *Mascara Literary Review*, *Cyclamen and Swords*, *Blue Fifth Review* and others. She was nominated for the Best of the Net Awards in 2011. She has given multiple readings nationally.

JOY C. AL-SOFI is a published writer of poetry, fiction and nonfiction. She was a Third-Prize winner in the Inaugural Proverse Poetry Prize Competition. Originally from the USA, she has been teaching English in Hong Kong since 2004. Her newest passion is making videos.

ART ALLEN is originally from Manchester, England. He grew up in Cheshire and completed a Masters in Creative Writing at the University of Oxford. During that time, his father died very suddenly and the poetry following that loss was collected into his début pamphlet, *Here Birds Are*, published by Green Bottle Press, London 2017. Poems from the collection won the *Madison Review Prize* and *The Mississippi Review Prize* 2017, and featured in the *Amsterdam Quarterly*, *The Irish Literary Review*, *The Bombay Review*, and *The Indian Review*. His poetry has also appeared previously in *Elbow Room*, *Eyot*, *Cactus Heart Review*, *Wilderness House* and *Vayavya*.

INDRAN AMIRTHANAYAGAM has published 13 poetry collections thus far, written in English, Spanish, French, and Haitian Creole. His latest include *Il n'est de solitude que l'île lointaine*, *Ventana Azul*, and *Uncivil War*. He writes on poetry and the arts.

SOLOMON AU YEUNG is currently an in-service teacher, in his third year at a local primary school in Tai O, Lantau Island. He finished his high school education at the Diocesan Boys' School, Hong Kong, and his undergraduate studies (in Risk

Management and Business Intelligence) at Hong Kong University of Science and Technology (HKUST). For his postgraduate study, apart from taking a PGDE in EdUHK, he is taking a part-time Master's programme offered by the University of Oxford, in Learning and Teaching. Solomon likes to explore various issues that relate to Education, both in the local setting and internationally. Recently, he discovered a new interest, writing poems: it seems a good way for him to relax. At the time of writing, three of his works are scheduled for publication.

SUI PING AU YEUNG is a poet, editor and poetry translator. Her poetry has appeared in several magazines like *Voice & Verse Poetry Magazine*, *Off the Roll*, *Poetry+* and *Qiu Ying Shi Kan*. Between 2012 and 2017, she was one of the editors of *Voice & Verse Poetry Magazine*.

THEA BIESHEUVEL was born in The Netherlands and migrated to Australia as a teenager. She wrote in Dutch at first, before honing her English language skills. She has had individual poems published by magazines. Her short stories have also attracted attention. She is now a tutor at The University of the Third Age (Brisbane, Australia) and enjoys a busy retirement.

MARÍA ELENA BLANCO (Havana, Cuba) Poet, essayist and translator, writes predominantly in her native Spanish. Having spent a good part of her formative years in New York, she translates her own poetry into English and has also developed her own English poetic voice in a style quite distinguishable from her Spanish one. Has taught French literature and language and worked for the United Nations as translator/reviser, presently on a freelance basis. She is a frequent participant in international literary events and a member of Labyrinth, the Association of English-Speaking Poets in Vienna. Her published work includes poetry collections *Posesión por pérdida* (Sevilla and Santiago, Chile, 1990), *Corazón sobre la tierra / tierra en los Ojos* (Cuba, 1998), *Alquímica memoria* (Madrid, 2001), *Mitologuías* (Madrid, 2001), *danubiomediterráneo /mittelmeerdonau* (Vienna, 2005, Spanish-German), *El amor incontable* (Madrid,

2008), *Havanity / Habanidad* (Miami, 2010, English-Spanish), *Escrito en lenguas* (Chile, 2015), *Sobresalto al vacío* (Chile, 2015) and *Botín* (Leiden, 2016), as well as a book of literary criticism, *Asedios al texto literario* (Madrid, 1999), and a volume of critical essays on Cuban culture and politics, *Devoraciones. Ensayos de período especial* (Leiden, 2016). She has also published Spanish translations of French and Austrian poets, among others. She resides mainly in Vienna, Austria, with periodic stays in Santiago, Chile.

STEVE BORST is a retired biomedical researcher and professor from Gainesville, Florida and has published many poems and stories over the years.

PAOLA CARONNI is from Milan, Italy and has been living in Asia since 1995. She is a freelance translator and tutor of the Italian language, a very involved Vice-President of the charity organisation, 'The Italian Women's Association', and writes poetry and fiction. She holds an MFA in Creative Writing from the University of Hong Kong and an MA in English Language and Literature from the University of Milan. Paola's poems have been included in various poetry collections—*Desde Hong Kong: Poets in Conversation with Octavio Paz*, *Quixotica: Poems East of La Mancha*, *Mingled Voices 2*—and have appeared in 'Voice and Verse Poetry Magazine', and *Cha, an Asian Literary Journal*.

One of Paola's short stories was selected and published on the 'PEN Hong Kong' website.

Since 2014, Paola has regularly contributed articles, fiction and poetry to the cultural platform, "Beyond Thirty-nine".

JOSIE CHAMBERS lives in the United Kingdom, where she co-ordinates the work funded by an educational charity, whose focus is the process of achievement, in individuals and in organisations. She was awarded the MBE in the 2011 Queen's Birthday Honours for services to Higher Education. When invited, she shares her poems with friends, colleagues and, in public readings with wider audiences, but has not, until recently, contemplated publishing her poems.

CAROL FLAKE CHAPMAN, a former journalist, returned to writing poetry after the death of her husband on a wild river in Guatemala. She has found poetry to be the language of healing and discovery. Because she lives in a place that has been battered by hurricanes, turning ordinary people into refugees, and because she lives close to a border where many refugees seek safety, she was attracted by the theme of refuge.

LAURIANE CHAPPE heads her commentary, "—From physical landscapes to inner landscapes...". She writes that she is a geographer by training (Master's degree of Geography and postgraduate diploma in Planning), and was first interested in the way in which natural elements as well as human history leave their imprints on the world and thus shape it.

Her career in management positions in communications, public relations and business development has also allowed her to observe closely interpersonal relationships and their stakes. After learning a lot about personal development, she felt ready to accompany people in search of evolution and well-being. Magnetizer of family tradition (grandfather magnetizer), she is now a practitioner in quantum therapies.

From now on, she uses writing (storytelling or poetry) to be aimed at everyone's heart, to encourage letting go and approach other realities.

PEI-KAI CHENG, Yale PhD in history, taught at the State University of New York, Yale, and Pace University, before founding the Chinese Civilization Center at the City University of Hong Kong in 1998. Awarded Merit of Honour by the Government of the Hong Kong SAR in 2016, he is now Chairman of the Hong Kong Intangible Cultural Heritage Consultation Committee.

He has published more than thirty books, covering various academic subjects such as Tang Xianzu, transcultural aesthetics, tea culture, Chinese export porcelain, and the English translation of Chinese classics. He founded the *Chinese Culture Quarterly* in 1986 and has been its Editor-in-chief ever since.

BENNY CHIA is the founder and director of the Fringe Club, a contemporary arts space he converted from a disused cold storage depot and shop-house. He has also launched and directed three alternative arts festivals in Hong Kong over three and a half decades. He is a published author of short stories and stage plays in English and Chinese. He started writing the odd poem during university for poetry competitions and susceptible girls. He revived his interest in writing poetry two years ago, rereading a poem by Cesar Vallejo while in Paris. Last year he sent four of his poems to Proverse which have been included in that year's anthology.

HELEN DAVIS comes from West Wales, an area where the sea is never far away. She is interested in Amnesty, art, comedy, literacy, music, people's poetry and tall tales. She likes to wander round at will , mostly in Hong Kong's Wanchai district or up the Peak. She enjoys Hong Kong on the whole, having lived there for eighteen years, mostly reading books with six to eight year olds or getting over-stimulated by this amazing place.

BRUCE LOUIS DODSON is an expatriate living in Borlänge, Sweden, where he practices photography and writes fiction and poetry. Some of his most recent work has appeared in: Breadline Press West Coast Poetry Anthology, *Foreign & Far Away*—Writers Abroad Anthology, Sleeping Cat Books—*Trip of a Lifetime* Anthology, *The Crucible*, *Northern Liberties Review*, *Pirene's Fountain*, *Sounds of Solace*—Meditative Verse Anthology, *Tic Toc* Anthology—Kind of a Hurricane Press, *High Coupe*, *Vine Leaves*, *Cordite Poetry Review*, *Buffalo Almanac*, *Madness Muse*, *Maintenant*, *Along The Shore*—Lost Tower Publications, *So It Goes*—Kurt Vonnegut Museum & Library, *Whitefish Review*, Smoky Blue Lit & Arts, *Permafrost*, *Art Ascent,* and *Popshot*.

After thirty years as a teacher of English Literature JOHN DORRELL moved from London to Asia, to work in schools, write and dream. He often writes about the experiences of leaving and finding identity from a mixed culture, and loves to play with poetic form and expectations.

NEIL DOUGLAS is a retired General Practitioner (GP) currently working in Community Paediatrics in London, United

Kingdom. He performs regularly for the London Writers Eclective and has been writing poetry for three years. He received a commendation in the Hippocrates International Prize 2018 and two of his poems appeared in *The North Magazine* in August 2018.

HASAN ERKEK, as a poet, a playwright and a professor of drama, has been awarded more than twenty national and international prizes. He has published twenty-five artistic and scientific books in thirteen different countries. His poetry books have been published in Turkey, France, Bulgaria and Romania. Some of his poems have been set to music by different composers from different countries. His works in his academic career have focused on the art of drama. His plays have been performed by more than forty theatres in different countries, including primarily Turkish national theatres. Furthermore, he has written radio plays (approximately 20 radio plays have been broadcast by national radios in Turkey) and film scripts (some of them have been filmed). One of his specialised fields is theatre for children. Hasan Erkek has taken part and presented papers in many international theatre festivals and symposia. He has had more than a hundred articles published in various journals and newspapers. He has given play reading, dramaturgy, dramatization, creative writing, drama techniques and contemporary theatre courses in various departments of various universities. Hasan Erkek has worked as an Executive Board Member and Vice-president of ASSITEJ Turkey, and has been president of the Turkish Playwrights and Play Translators Association as well as the Head of the Department of Performing Arts at Anadolu University.

HILARY FAULKNER was born in the United Kingdom and first came to Hong Kong in 1987 to join her older brother. She unfortunately returned to the UK in 1997 for health reasons, which escalated in 2014. She moved back in 2012 from their family home in Bath, UK and her mother joined her in 2013. She loves the Asian culture scene and she and her family regularly participate in the annual Hong Kong Arts Festival. She has now lived in Asia on and off for 30 years. She has travelled extensively throughout the region with her job and was stationed in Singapore for a year.

Her mother emigrated to Hong Kong at the age of 85 to be closer to her two children since her husband, Hilary's father, passed away in 1989.

Hilary and her mother have always had a love of books and reading and belonged to several book clubs in the UK, including that of the British Federation of University Women (now the British Federation of Women Graduates), where they initially heard about the Proverse Prize for Poetry. Hilary has also joined the Hong Kong Association of University Women.

In 2014 Hilary was diagnosed with a rare aggressive form of Ovarian Cancer which has now spread to stage 4 and she is on palliative care. She is currently writing a book to share her cancer journey to help and support other women with this disease. The cancer research and care in Hong Kong is so advanced that she is doing very well on her treatment and wants to share all the expertise she has learned.

MICHAEL GOULD is a Canadian New Zealander, resident in Wellington for the past 25 years. His book, *Surrealism and the Cinema: Open-eyed Screening*, was published in 1976, but by then he had turned to writing poetry; some published in Canada in the late seventies; he then stopped submitting his writing for almost four decades. His new poetry is appearing in various Australasian publications, including *Landfall*, *The Spinoff*, *Meniscus*, *Snorkel*, *The Café Reader* and *Otoliths*.

ELIZABETH GROBLER is from South Africa and has a B.Ed. Honours degree in Learning Support, Guidance and Counselling. She moved to South Korea in 2006 and arrived in Hong Kong in 2010. Several of her poems and short stories have been published in anthologies in Hong Kong. Elizabeth has been teaching at a primary school on HK Island for almost nine years where she enjoys developing curriculum as well as writing and directing plays and musicals for stage and Campus TV productions.

D.J. HAMILTON has written plays, poetry and essays. He previously worked in professional theatre as an actor, director and playwright. For the last 15 years he has worked as a teacher. He has taught Literature, Drama, Theatre, Speech and English Language Acquisition. He currently teaches Drama and lives in Hong Kong with his wife, Montserrat Salazar.

MATTHEW SCOTT HARRIS (the second offspring and only son of Boyce and the late Harriet Harris) made his unheralded debut on a brutally cold (predating fierce Polar Vortex) January thirteenth.

Once awareness blossomed within the iris of each eye, Mother Nature with proclivity to become most grounded when basking in the seasonal pastel of sounds and aromas wafting from postage stamp size of suburban residences parents (particularly his whip smart ambitious mechanical engineered college trained dada) relocated the young family.

This contemplative, elective, furtive predilection arose and stemmed from self-propelled exposure to fauna and flora. All creatures great and small found him bedazzled, delighted, fixated, harmonized, kindled, moored, ogled, quelled, seduced, tantalized, vaunted from biodiversity.

His father (as iterated above spent his working career employed as a mechanical engineer with General Electric), heard the powerful lungs of this gangly newborn, which precluded the need for an alarm clock.

This little sportive whippersnapper born in Cincinnati, Ohio, yet lived the majority of a current lick-spittle existence within Southeastern Montgomery County, Pennsylvania.

Extreme shyness in tandem with a congenital speech defect (submucous cleft palate) seemed to alienate him from other classmates. Additionally such genetic mutation evinced a pronounced nasality, an ideal trait which bullies found a perfect cause for nasty teasing and tormenting.

As an outside neutral observer, I watched with gut wrenching agony how he seemed socially detached and rarely invited to join in any reindeer games.

Yes, a gross degree of taunting left him without friends. Lack of confidence and ultra reticence offered manna to brawny bad ass brutes. Matter of fact, this vulnerability and susceptibility being the receiving end of verbal slings continued all thru public education.

JONATHAN LOCKE HART is Chair Professor, Creative Writing, Comparative Literature, Theory, and Literature in English and Director, Centre for Creative Writing and Literary Translation and Culture at Shanghai Jiao Tong University. He is also Core Faculty in Comparative Literature at Western University and Life Member, Clare Hall, University of Cambridge. A Fellow of the Royal Society of Canada, he is a poet, writer of other genres, literary scholar and historian who studied at Toronto and Cambridge and has held visiting appointments at Harvard, Cambridge, Princeton, Toronto, the Sorbonne Nouvelle (Paris III) and elsewhere. The author of many articles and over twenty books, including *Theater and World* (1992), *Northrop Frye: The Theoretical Imagination* (1994) and *The Poetics of Otherness* (2015), he has been writing since he was thirteen, and, for more than thirty years, his poetry has appeared in literary journals, such as *Quarry, Grain, The Antigonish Review, Mattoid* and *Harvard Review*. His books of poetry include, *Breath and Dust, Dream China* and *The Burning Lake*, out with Proverse in Hong Kong in late November 2016.

STEVEN HARZ is the author of multiple collections of love stories and is a multi-time winner of The Iron Writer Challenge. Originally from West Virginia, he grew up in Maryland, and now lives in New England.

His series, "Backroad Love Stories," covers various topics and moves between stories that, on one end of the spectrum resemble the lyrics of a country love song, to the other end where his words cut into the reader, reminding them of the pain caused by loves gained and lost.

Steven Harz is a graduate of Towson University's College of Fine Arts and Communication. He loves music and reading, coffee and Dr Pepper, sports and Broadway, and watching his boys perform on stage and the baseball diamond.

Steven's words have been highlighted in Inwood Indiana Press' Tracks, *The Pangolin Review, Voices 2, Donut Factory, Words+Pictures, Amethyst Review, Ink Monkey Magazine, The Germ, The Voices Project, Pocket Thoughts*, and *Indigo Rising UK*.

KATE HAWKINS is a TV presenter, actor, voice artist, poet, and published writer living in Hong Kong, where she spent much of her childhood. She has written scripts for television, is a published poet and is currently writing her first feature film. She co-edited two Hong Kong Writers Circle anthologies, *Another Hong Kong* and *Hong Kong Gothic*. She had poems published in the 2017 Proverse poetry anthology *Mingled Voices 2*, as well as having work published in previous Hong Kong Writers Circle anthologies. She holds a degree in Creative Writing from Queensland University of Technology in Brisbane, Australia and has been writing for as long as she can remember.

STEPHEN HERMAN has an MFA in Creative Writing/Poetry, U. Mass., Amherst . He taught Creative Writing/Poetry for 12 years at the City College of San Francisco. His *Night Visions* was Published in 2012, and awarded the Gold Seal of Literary Excellence First Prize in Poetry, 2013. He has been SF Writers' Conference SF Human Rights Commissioner for two years.

ANTONY HUEN has published poems and articles in *Cha: An Asian Literary Journal*, *The Compass Magazine*, *Eborakon*, *The Ekphrastic Review*, *The Shanghai Literary Review*, *Voice & Verse Poetry Magazine*, and elsewhere. He was one of Eyewear Publishing's Best New British and Irish Poets in 2017. At the University of York, he is a PhD candidate in the Department of English and Related Literature, and was appointed as a doctoral fellow of the Humanities Research Centre.

JADE HUI is a final-year student at The University of Hong Kong studying Philosophy, Comparative Literature and Counseling. She's concerned and confused about how humans should live, and hopes to be educated through interdisciplinary training and research.

Canadian poet AKIN JEJE lives in Hong Kong. An active poet and spoken-word performer, Jeje's works have been published and featured in Canada and Hong Kong. Jeje's first work, *Dreaming of The Sands* was published in Canada in 1999. His first full-length poetry collection, *Smoked Pearl: Poems of*

Hong Kong and Beyond was a semi-finalist for the 2009 International Proverse Prize, and was published by Proverse Hong Kong in 2010.

Jeje's work was also featured in the collaborative poem 'A poem for Jack Layton', by 14 Canadian Poets, published in Canada's *The Globe and Mail* newspaper, 26 August 2011, and his most recent publication was in Hong Kong's Chameleon Press anthology, *Quixotica; Poems East of La Mancha* (July 2016). Jeje has also published in other Hong Kong and Canadian publications such as *fifty-fifty*, *Asian Cha*, *Carousel*, *Outloud Too* and *Filling Station*. Jeje's most recent publication, "Reach" was in the Voice and Verse-Cha Tenth Anniversary Special Feature magazine (March 2018). He is currently at work on another full-length poetry collection tentatively entitled "never land".

For almost a decade Jeje has been a regular performer at Hong Kong's monthly Poetry Outloud event. In addition, from 2007 to 2014, he served as the MC for Hong Kong's Peel Street Poetry collective, and is still a core member of the group. He was an advisor to the Hong Kong International Young Readers' Festival, and was a volunteer moderator for the Hong Kong International Literary Festival from 2012 to 2016. Jeje has performed his poetry for public events and in schools, and has been presenting educational seminars on poetry for primary and secondary school students since 2014.

MEGHAN KELSEY earned her MFA from Arizona State University. She teaches in Phoenix, AZ.

ZACHARY TAYLOR KNOX's poems have appeared in *Ealain*, *Penny Ante Feud*, *Scum Gentry*, and *What Rough Beast*. He lives in Fort Madison, Iowa with his family.

CHRISTOS KOUKIS is a Greek poet and writer, born and raised in Athens, Greece. He has published poetry books in Greece, France, Serbia, Germany and India. He has participated in many international poetry festival in Europe and Asia and his poems have been translated into several languages. He has worked in art magazines and has been a poet for an international project of Documenta14.

FRANZ KRABEL has been writing poems all his life. He writes that it is one of his many passions.

CAROL PARRIS KRAUSS is a mother, high school teacher, and poet from the Tidewater region of Virginia. She enjoys gardening and spending time with her many pets. Her work has been published in many online and print journals such as *Poetry24*, *The Amsterdam Quarterly*, *Storysouth*, *New Verse News*, and *Blue Collar Review*.

LYNDA MCKINNEY LAMBERT is the author of two full-length books: *Concerti: Psalms for the Pilgrimage*, Kota Press, 2003 and *Walking by Inner Vision: Stories & Poems*, DLD Books, 2017. She was nominated: "Skirt Best of the Net 2017" for her essay, 'Knitting a Life Back Together,' published in *Spirit Fire Review*. Her poem, 'Red December' won a poetry publication prize and was published in *Mingled Voices 2*, Proverse Hong Kong, 2017. Lynda's career is featured in, *Artful Alchemy*, ed. Anne Copeland. DLD Books, 2017. Lynda's work appears in *Indiana Voice Journal*; *Spirit Fire Review*, *Magnets & Ladders*, *Breath & Shadow*, *Poetry Quarterly*, *Tana Society of America*, *Tanka Journal*, *Plum Tree Tavern*, *NatureWriting*, *The Avocet*, *Plinth*, *blue Unicorn*, *Pro Christo*, *Proteus*, *No Limits*, *Kaleidoscope*, *Wordgathering*, and more.

Lynda loves rural life; standing in a meadow of wild flowers and thistles; gazing into a midnight sky; long winters; walks in the woods at daylight; solitary days with her husband, Bob, two rescued cats and two rescued dogs.

SUSAN LAVENDER is a published poet, actress, solicitor, radio newsreader, Italian translator and regular participant at Poetry Outloud, Peel St. Poetry and Liars' League HK. She performs poetry, in theatre, and other spoken word events, often writing her own material. Anglo-Italian by birth, she is bilingual in English and Italian, fluent in French and she has degrees in law and modern languages. She is a registered interpreter/translator at the Italian Consulate in Hong Kong and has worked as an advisor (English/Italian) for the Hong Kong Academy of Performing Arts. She has also learnt Romanian and Chinese. She studied Mandarin in Beijing in the nineties.

She studied acting in the UK in the seventies before going to university and it has remained her first love which she has never deserted throughout her life.

JEMIMA LAW is an undergraduate business student who has had an interest in writing and visual arts for as long as she can remember. To her, they serve as an outlet for her emotions when she doesn't quite understand what she's feeling yet, or when she has no one to talk to. As a shy and self conscious individual, writing and art have always allowed her to understand herself in ways no one else could, and communicate the experiences she's had in a more meaningful manner. When she's not busy creating art or articulating her thoughts, she enjoys spending time with her family, eating good food, taking photos, exploring Hong Kong and watching movies.

HO CHEUNG LEE (Peter), Ed.D., is the founding editor of BALLOONS Lit. Journal. His second poetry chapbook *Something Celebrative or Immortal Under Another Birdless Sky* was published by Jamii Publishing in 2018. His work (poetry/short stories/photography) has appeared in *Rattle*, **82 Review*, *Shearsman Magazine*, *Interpreter's House*, *The Writing Disorder*, *The Oddville Press*, and elsewhere. His poetry was shortlisted in Oxford Brookes University's International Poetry Competition (2016), for erbacce-prize for poetry (2017) and The Proverse Poetry Prize (2017). He teaches English in Hong Kong.

ELBERT SIU PING LEE lives in Ontario, Canada. His poems have appeared in a number of anthologies, namely, *Fifty/Fifty: A new anthology of Hong Kong writing* and *Hong Kong Poems, an English German anthology*. His collection, *Rain on The Pacific Coast*, published by Proverse Hong Kong, 2013, was awarded support from the Hong Kong Arts Development Council. More recent work of his appears in the volumes *Quixotica—Poems East of La Mancha*, Chameleon Press, Hong Kong 2016 and *Twin Cities*, ed. Joshua Ip & Tammy Ho Lai-Wing, 2017.

LEUNG RACHEL KA YIN has just turned twenty, is a student of Psychology, and is currently on a Gap Semester. She was born and raised in Hong Kong and is now pursuing her studies at St Hilda's College, University of Oxford. She was formerly the Chief Editor and Contributor to the Poetry/ Short-story columns of Bou Zi, the school magazine of Li Po Chun United World College of Hong Kong, as well as Contributor to *Synergy*, the official publication of Li Po Chun United World College of Hong Kong. She is passionate about mental health issues, special needs education and feminism. In her free time, she enjoys writing poetry and non-fictional short stories.

SELENA LIANG is currently a student of the Chinese University of Hong Kong, majoring in Journalism and Communication. Since high school, she has developed an interest in writing and literature in English. She has often found herself disconnected from the majority of Hong Kong when it comes to English reading and writing. Recently, she has learnt more about Hong Kong Literature in English and aspires to be one of the contributors.

BIRGIT BUNZEL LINDER was born and raised in Oberhausen, an industrial city in the Ruhr Valley. She left Germany in the 1980s, and has since lived in Taiwan, China, America, and now in Hong Kong. She teaches Chinese and Comparative Literary Studies at Shandong University in China. She won the International Proverse Prize for Poetry in 2012 for her first collection, *Shadows in Deferment*, which contains poetry marked by frequent moves and many travels, and by inscriptions from different places, cultures, and people. Her second collection *Bliss of Bewilderment* (Proverse 2017) turns her encounters into spiritual journeys that begin in bewilderment and end in bliss. Birgit Bunzel Linder has previously published poems in *Mad Poets Review*, *Clockwise Cat*, *Kavya Bharati*, *Cerebration*, *International Literary Quarterly*, *Asian Cha*, *Lakeview International Journal of Literature and Arts*, and, among others, in *Poetry Against Terror: A Tribute to the Victims of Terrorism*. Besides writing, she likes painting, reading, and photography.

BELLE LING is a PhD student in Creative Writing, specializing in Poetry, at The University of Queensland, Australia. She likes writing poems which shuffle between the quotidian and the transcendent, provoking in-depth thoughts on philosophical reflection. Her poems have appeared in *Cha: An Asian Literary Journal*, *Barnwood International Poetry Magazine*, *Overland*, *Meanjin*, *Taj Mahal Review*, *The Istanbul Review* and more. Her poetry collection, "A Seed and a Plant" was shortlisted for The HKU International Poetry Prize 2010. Her poem, "That Space," won a second place in the ESL category of the International Poetry Competition organized by the Oxford Brookes University in October 2016. She was the recipient of the Playa Residency, Oregon, in 2014. She was awarded a Merit Scholarship at the New York State Summer Writers Institute in 2017. She is currently working on her dissertation on the relationship between food and poetry by looking at Pablo Neruda's food odes.

J.P. LINSTROTH has a D.Phil. in Social and Cultural Anthropology from the University of Oxford in the UK. He is also author of *Marching Against Gender Practice: Political Imaginings in the Basqueland* (Lexington Books, 2015). Linstroth's research interests include: ethnicity, nationalism, immigrant rights, indigenous rights, indigenous politics, gender, genocide, terrorism, peace studies, peace building, cognition, memory, trauma, immigrant rights, and social justice. He published his first book of poetry, *The Forgotten Shore* (Poetic Matrix Press), in 2017.

JACK MAYER is a Vermont writer and pediatrician. His was the first pediatric practice in Eastern Franklin County, on the Canadian border, where he began writing essays, poems and short stories about his practice and hiking Vermont's Long Trail. He was a country doctor for ten years, often bartering medical care for eggs, firewood, and knitted afghans. From 1987 to 1991 Dr Mayer was a National Cancer Institute Fellow at Columbia University researching the molecular biology of cancer. In 1991 Dr Mayer established Rainbow Pediatrics in Middlebury, Vermont, where he continues to practice primary care pediatrics. He is an Instructor in Pediatrics at the University of Vermont School of Medicine and an adjunct faculty for pre-medical students at Middlebury College. He was a participant at the Bread Loaf Writers' Conference in 2003 and 2005 (fiction) and 2008 (poetry). His first non-fiction book is *Life In A Jar: The Irena Sendler Project*. Dr Mayer's new book, *Before The Court Of Heaven*, is historical fiction and has received 14 book awards. His poem, 'I Am A God To The Birds' won First Prize in the 2017 Proverse Poetry contest.

AYA MOHTADI was born in a small Lebanese town in 1998. Her ardent passion for literature sprung at an early age and led to the English Literature major she is still pursuing at the Lebanese University. She functions off coffee and sleep deprivation. She composes most of her works at 3am. She loves animals, nature, and serial-killer stories. Her poem 'Confessions of an Orphan in Fear' emanated from the belief that ephemeral experiences can be eternized internally.

Besides being a freelance writer and poetry enthusiast, LONNIE MONKA runs Jerusalism (jerusalism.com), an initiative to foster local literary community through reading series, author meet ups, workshops, and more. Lonnie currently studies art theory and policy at Bezalel Academy, writes reviews of local exhibitions, and regularly contributes to Contemporary Art in Jerusalem (caij.co).

RONY NAIR is a poet, photographer and a part time columnist. A Briton of Indian descent, his professional photography has been exhibited and also been featured in several literary journals. His poetry, photography and writings have previously been featured by the *Chiron Review*, *Modern Literature*, *The Indian Express*, *Quail Bell Magazine*, *YGDRASIL journal*, *Mindless Muse*, *Yellow Chair Review*, *Two Words For*, *Alephi*, *New Asian Writing* (NAW), *Semaphore*, The Economic Times, *1947*, *The Foliate Oak Magazine*, *Open Road Magazine*, *Tipton Review*, *Antarctica Journal*, *North East Review*, *Indian Literature*, and *Coldnoon*, among many others. Rony has exhibited his art widely and continues to work on his non-fiction and poetry projects.

TY NEWCOMB lives in Lake Charles, Louisiana with his wife Brianna and their two cats. He currently works at the public library, but will soon be heading to an MFA program at Minnesota State University. He's been published in *Luminous Echoes*, a collection by Into the Void, as well as in *Stonecoast*

Review, *Sagebrush Review*, and *Marathon Literary Review*. He enjoys collecting and keeping beetles.

When people move from one place to another, it is not uncommon to experience loneliness and life stressors. N. NOELL finds healing through writing to achieve inner peace, completeness and security. As a digital nomad who keeps blogging and un-blogging, Noell never stops writing. The child of Asian immigrants, Noell has worked as a journalist, teacher and operation manager.

KEITH NUNES lives in tiny Pahiatua (New Zealand). He won the 2017 Flash Frontier Short Fiction Writing Award, has been published around the globe, placed in competitions and been a Pushcart Prize nominee. His Foto-Poetry digital images have appeared in a number of literary journals. His book of poetry/short fiction, *catching a ride on a paradox*, is sold widely in NZ.

PATIENCE O'NEILL likes to listen, reflect and imagine. She has taught and counselled people, and now writes for pleasure. She is fascinated by dialogue and people's way of expressing themselves. She enjoys travel.

JUN (JANICE) PAN is an interpreter, translator, researcher and interpreter and translator trainer. With a passion for reading and writing, she founded a Chinese poetry club and published a couple of Chinese poems (*shi* and *ci*) at the age of twelve at her birthplace in Xiangtan, Hunan. She then studied English language and literature in Jiangsu and interpreting in Shanghai. She came to Hong Kong in 2008 for her PhD on interpreting studies and has been teaching interpreting and translation at local tertiary institutions since then.

Jun has worked as an interpreter (and translator) for many years, although her childhood dream was to become a writer, director or painter. She found her childhood immersion in Chinese classic literature and culture important and invaluable in her life and career. Apart from introducing Chinese culture to many of her clients when she worked as an interpreter, Jun also participated in the translation of several classic works from English to Chinese, including John Ruskin's five-volumed

Modern Painters, Lyman Frank Baum's *The Wonderful Wizard of Oz* and *The Marvelous Land of Oz*.

Jun is now Associate Professor in the Translation Programme and Director of the M.A. Programme in Translation and Bilingual Communication at Hong Kong Baptist University. She has also been playing *Guqin* (the Chinese seven-stringed zither) during the past seven years, which, according to her, helps her to find an inner peace in her constant struggle and search for a balance between an oriental and occidental cultural identity.

SUSAN PHILLIPS is a British Crime Historian with a background in mental health and criminal law. She is in the process of completing her first non-fiction book about a real-life murder that occurred in 1914. She is also collecting oral histories about the workers who built the Spitfire aircraft in Southampton in World War Two and these narratives will be stored for posterity in the Southampton city archives.

DANNY POON is teaching English in a secondary school in Hong Kong. He was inspired to write when he pursued his first degree in English Language and Literature at Hong Kong Baptist University from 1996-1999. During this period of time, he served as the Chief Editor for his Department Journal. He obtained a Master's degree in Intercultural Studies from The Chinese University of Hong Kong in 2005. He has kept writing ever since, hoping to get his poems published one day.

ROCHELLE POTKAR is author of *The Arithmetic of Breasts and other stories* and *Four Degrees of Separation*, Rochelle Potkar is an alumna of Iowa's International Writing Program and Charles Wallace Writer's fellowship, Stirling.

She is the winner of the 2016 Open Road Review story contest for 'The leaves of the deodar'. Her story 'Chit Mahal' (The Enclave) appears in *The Best of Asian Short Stories*. Her poem 'Place' won an honorable mention at *Asian Cha*'s Auditory Cortex. Her poem 'The girl from Lal Bazaar' was shortlisted for the Gregory O'Donoghue International Poetry Prize, 2018. Her latest book of prose poems is *Paper Asylum* (Copper Coin Publishing, May 2018). Her poem, 'Skirt', has been adapted into a poetry film by Philippa Collie Cousins (UK), for the Visible Poetry Project 2018, USA.

SIMONA RACKOVÁ (b. 1976) is a poet, editor, literary critic and journalist. She graduated with an MA in Czech Language and Literature at the Philosophical Faculty of the Charles University in Prague. Since 2013, she has been the head editor of the Review Department at the prestigious art and literary magazine *Tvar*. She also edited an annual publication *Sto nejlepších českých básní* 2012 (One Hundred Best Czech Poems; Host Publishers) and the two-volume Antologie české poezie in 2007 and 2009 respectively (An Anthology of Czech Poetry; dybbuk Publishers). Her debut poetry collection *Přítelkyně* (Girlfriends; in the Literární salon Publisher, Prague) came out in 2007. Her collection of twelve poems about Venice, *Město, které není* (A City that Doesn't Exist), accompanied by linocuts of Pavel Piekar, was printed privately as a small-run publication in 2009. It was followed by the 2015 collection *Tance* (Dances, Dauphin Publ., Prague). She is the 2016 winner of the international Dresden Lyrical Prize. The presented poems come from the collection *Tance*. Simona's latest collection *Zatímco hlídací psi spí* was published in September 2017 (While the Guard Dogs Are Asleep; Dauphin Publ., Prague). She lives with her husband and two children in Prague.

JOANNA RADWAŃSKA-WILLIAMS was born in Warsaw, Poland, and spent a part of her childhood in London, England. She received her B.A. with a double major in English and Linguistics (awarded with Highest Honours, 1981) and her Ph.D. in Linguistics (1989) from the University of North Carolina at Chapel Hill. Her dissertation was published as *Paradigms Lost: The Linguistic Theory of Mikołaj Kruszewski* (Amsterdam: John Benjamins, 1993). Her research interests include the history of linguistics, language teaching methodology, poetics, semiotics, intercultural communication, and interdisciplinary applications of linguistics, and she has authored or co-authored over forty journal articles and book chapters in these fields. She is currently the General Editor of *Intercultural Communication Studies*, the official journal of the International Association for Intercultural Communication

Studies.

Joanna has taught Slavic Linguistics at the State University of New York at Stony Brook (1989-1994) and the University of Illinois at Chicago (1994-1995), and English Linguistics at Nanjing University (1996-1999) and the Chinese University of Hong Kong (1999-2003). In 2003, she joined Macao Polytechnic Institute, where she has served as a Professor of English in the School of Business, the School of Languages and Translation and the MPI-Bell Centre of English.

Joanna's poetry has been anthologized in several collections, including *Lingua Franca: An Anthology of Poetry by Linguists* (edited by Donna Jo Napoli and Emily Norwood Rando; Lake Bluff, Illinois: Jupiter Press, 1989), *Montage of Life* (Owings Mills, Maryland: The National Library of Poetry, 1998), *I Roll the Dice: Contemporary Macao Poetry* (edited by Christopher Kit Kelen and Agnes Vong; Macao: Association of Stories in Macao, 2008), and *Mingled Voices 2: International Proverse Poetry Prize Anthology 2017* (edited by Gillian Bickley and Verner Bickley; Hong Kong: Proverse Hong Kong, 2018).

PATRICK T. REARDON is the author of eight books, including *Requiem for David*, a poetry collection, and *Faith Stripped to Its Essence*, a literary-religious analysis of Shusaku Endo's novel, *Silence*. Reardon, a former reporter with the *Chicago Tribune*, has had poetry published in a variety of in-print and online journals, including *Silver Birch Press, Cold Noon, Eclectica, Ground Fresh Thursday, Literary Orphans, Rhino, Spank the Carp, Time for Singing, Tipton Poetry Journal, Under a Warm Green Linden* and *The Write City*.

M. ANN REED is a contemplative scholar, poet, Chinese calligrapher-brush painter and professor of English Literature and Theory of Knowledge. She has taught in Malaysia, Ukraine, Bosnia-Herzegovina and China. Her postdoctoral research studies the mending arts of Early Modern English and Contemporary Poetry. Her Chinese calligraphy and brush paintings have been exhibited in Portland, Oregon and at the Shenzhen Fine Arts Museum in China. Her poems have been published in various literary journals. She is the co-recipient of the Lazuli Literary Group 2018 poetry prize.

VINNI RELWANI lives in Singapore, calling it home for the last twenty years, with a soft-spot for Hong Kong where she was born and raised. A homemaker and mum, Vinni enjoys writing, and is in her zone when writing poetry and short stories.

ANGELO RIZZI was born in 1956, in Sant'Angelo Lodigiano, Italy. His mother tongue is Italian, but he is a polyglot poet, writing in Arabic, Italian and French. He has published fourteen collections of poems, the most recent being, *Lemhat al-hidâ'ati* (bilingual) (The profile of the kite), ed. BoD, 2018.

He has received many literary awards, such as the prestigious Nosside World Prize in 2004. In 2016, the Academia Internacional de Ciências, Létras and Art ALPAS XXI in Cruz Alta (Porto Alegre), R/S Brazil, nominated him International Correspondent Academic.

He has participated in international poetry meetings in Rome (Italy), Havana (Cuba), Paris (France), Curtea de Argeş (Romanía) and Djerba (Tunisia). In 2006, he attended the UNESCO Congress, "Dialogue among the Nations".

Rizzi is a member of REMES (Red Mundial de Escritores en Español); World Poets Society; Poetas del Mundo and SELAE (Sociedad de Escritores Latino-Americanos y Europeos).

His poems have appeared in anthologies and magazines in Italy, the United States, Switzerland, Cuba, Argentina, Spain, Kuwait, Brazil, Romania, Hong Kong, and India.

HALIL SUAT SARAÇ is twenty-two years old, studying psychology in Turkey. His passions are human beings and writing their story. He wishes to become a playwright and put his plays on stage one day. He knows how to speak and write English and Turkish. He is also interested in learning French and Spanish to be better able to understand the poetry of these languages.

SANJA SÄRMAN is a woman of Sino-Swedish descent. She has two Bachelor Degrees (one in literature and one in philosophy), and one master's degree (philosophy), all three obtained at Uppsala University in Sweden, where she also studied various ancient and modern languages.

At the time of writing, she is enrolled as a PhD student at the University of Hong Kong, where she explores moral and literary issues in early modern and late modern philosophy.

She has studied visual arts (drawing and painting) at The Royal Academy of Fine Arts in Brussels and Yunnan Art Institute in China. She mostly paints mythological motifs and portraits.

JOSE MANUEL SEVILLA was born in Barcelona in 1959. His poetry books published (in Spanish) are: *From the limits of paradise (*1991), *Alice in Ikea's Catalogue* and *The Night of Europe* (2004).

In 2009, he was awarded the Angel Urrutia poetry award for, *Ashes of Auschwitz and Eighteen Dogs*. His book, *Family Album*, was published in 2016.

His plays for the theatre are: "The Bridge" (written after a trip to Croatia during the last European war, and staged in Catalonia, Spain (2000) and Hong Kong (2011), "Sombras, Sol y Flamenco" (Ballet by Ingrid Sera-Gilet, Hong Kong) and "Kennedy" 2016.

His poem, 'Sonia Wants to Rent an Apartment' won first prize in the Asian Cha Poetry Contest, "Encountering", in 2012 . His group of poems, "Of Words and Keys" was included in the Proverse Prize 2017 anthology *Mingled Voices 2*, and his poem, 'Voice and Verse', in the *Asian Cha* Tenth Anniversary Anthology.

ALLEGRA JOSTAD SILBERSTEIN grew up on a farm in Wisconsin but has lived in California since 1963. Her love of poetry began as a child when her mother would recite poems as she worked. Now that she is retired there is more time for singing and dancing as well as poetry. She has three chapbooks of poetry. In the spring of 2015, Cold River Press published her first book and she is widely published in journals such as *Blue Unicorn*, *California Quarterly*, *Iodine Poetry* and *Poetry Now*. In March of 2010 she was honoured to become the first Poet Laureate for the city of Davis, CA.

HAYLEY ANN SOLOMON is an award winning New Zealand author, librarian and poet. She writes an eclectic mix of fantasy fiction, historical romance, literary short stories and poetry.

LAURA SOLOMON is the author of fourteen books, nine of which are in the University of Oxford. Her books are in over 120 libraries worldwide. Her publishers are Proverse Hong Kong, Woven Words India and Creativia, Finland.

JEDDIE SOPHRONIUS was born in Jakarta, Indonesia. He is a senior at Western Michigan University, majoring in English with an emphasis in creative writing. His work has appeared or is forthcoming in *Bridge*, *Watershed Review*, *Juked*, *The Ear*, and *Relief*. He currently lives in Kalamazoo.

ANDREW SUTHERLAND is a writer, poet, and theatre-maker working between Perth and Singapore. He was awarded Overland's Fair Australia Poetry Prize 2017 for his work "East Perth [imagined nation]". Theatre works include Unveiling: Gay Sex for Endtimes, Baby Girl, Chrysanthemum Gate, and Ragnarok, all of which have had multiple iterations across Australia and in Singapore.

ABBIE JOHNSON TAYLOR is the author of a novel, two poetry collections, and a memoir. She's currently working on another novel. Her work has appeared in *The Weekly Avocet*, *Magnets and Ladders*, and other journals and anthologies. She has a visual impairment and lives in Sheridan, Wyoming, where for six years, she cared for her late husband, who was totally blind and partially paralyzed as a result of two strokes.

LUISA TERNAU was born in Trieste, Italy. Poetry has been part of her life since childhood. Luisa has lived and worked in several countries around the world. Currently she is based in Hong Kong.

EDWARD TIESSE was born and raised in Washington State. When he was a teenager, he discovered T.S. Elliot, W.B. Yeats and the Beat Poets. Thus began his life-long love of poetry. He was an English major who taught for a while, worked in the restaurant business where he trained chefs, and after graduate school, he worked as an organization development consultant for a large aerospace firm. Although his corporate job kept him fully occupied, he always found time to write poetry.

Edward has many interests. He loves to cook and recently began baking bread which he soon learned is much like writing poetry. That is, the combinations of flour, water and yeast have many variables and so baking is much like trying to find the right word and its place in a line. Edward's poetry has been published in *The Front Porch Review*, *The Sea Letter* and *Mingled Voices 2* (Proverse, 2017).

ROGER UREN has spent a long time in the diplomatic service, and is very conscious of the games played by politicians. He takes the view that the world would be much better if politicians were more focused on improving the world rather than promoting their own image.

PETER COE VERBICA grew up on a commercial cattle ranch in Northern California. He obtained a BA and JD from Santa Clara University and an MS from the Massachusetts Institute of Technology. He is married and has four daughters.

DAVID VOGNAR is a graduate of Northwestern University and the University of Chicago. He was the poetry editor of Northwestern's *Helicon* from 2006-2008. He is a social worker in Chicago.

OLGA WALLÓ's native tongue is Czech; a complicated minority language, precise and singing, of unsure future. Any translation is a postcard to far friends of global understanding.

ANSON HONGHUA WANG is an Assistant Professor in Translation. Her research interests are interpreter and translator training, gender and translation and second language acquisition. She is a practicing translator and interpreter. Besides research, she has a wide range of interests including reading, watching movies and hiking. She has been serving as Executive Committee Member of the Hong Kong Association of University Women since 2013. She is also a member of the

International Association for Translation and Intercultural Studies.

BRUCE ARLEN WASSERMAN assembled his first poetry manuscript at the age of seventeen and later farmed and worked as a blacksmith in his twenties. He received his MFA from Vermont College of Fine Arts. His poem, 'The Wet on Milan Street', was nominated for a Pushcart Prize. His poem, 'Elegy for My Father', appears in the Proverse Poetry Prize Anthology, 2017, and his short story, 'The Almost Living', was selected as a semi-finalist for the 2017 Francine Ringold Awards for New Writers. His poem, 'Louisiana Life', appears in the Spring/Summer, 2018 edition of *The Fredericksburg Literary and Art Review*. Bruce is a book critic for the *New York Journal of Books* and the *Washington Independent Review of Books* and a Graduate Assistant at the MFA in Writing program of Vermont College of Fine Arts. At other times, he creates visual art as a potter, performs as a musician in a band, trains horses on occasion and is a dentist in clinical practice.

GEORGE WATT has had teaching and administrative posts at universities in Australia, USA, Macau, and Japan and took up the writing of poetry at a very late stage in his life. Rather than diminish the importance of the act, it gives it some urgency and a very special poignancy.

RICHARD WESTLEY'S poems have appeared in *Cadence*, *riverrun*, *Tomorrow Magazine* and will appear in 'Deep Water' (Portland Press Herald) in the summer of 2018. Richard's novel, *B League Champs*, appeared in 2006; his audiobook narration of it has recently been released on Audible. His novella, *The Remarkable Conversion of Abdou Diouf* (Running Wild Press), will appear in July, 2018. Rich teaches creative writing for the Virtual High School. He lives in Kennebunk, Maine.

ELIZABETH WONG, popularly known as, "Libby", studied English at the University of Hong Kong, under the tutelage of Professor Edmund Charles Blunden, then Head of the English Department and British Poet Laureate. She graduated with a B.A. Hons. Degree, followed by a post-graduate diploma with distinction in Education. She also attended sponsored courses in New Zealand and at the Harvard Business School, USA, respectively.

A registered teacher in Hong Kong, she taught English before pursuing a career in the Administrative Service of the Hong Kong Government, serving in various key positions, including the following.

In the early 1980s, as Music Administrator, she promoted music and the performing arts and was instrumental in setting up the Academy for the Performing Arts (APA) in Hong Kong.

In 1987, as Director of the Social Welfare Department, she introduced major reforms, including the introduction of the Senior Citizens Card.

In 1990, she was appointed Secretary for Health and Welfare and was responsible for setting up the Hospital Authority (HA) in Hong Kong.

In 1995, she took early retirement from the civil service to go into politics. She was elected with the highest number of votes to Hong Kong's last Legislative Council under British rule in 1995.

In 1997, she quit politics to write. She has published novels, plays, poems and short stories. She has also worked with Hong Kong students on drama, poetry and creative writing.

She was a columnist with *Ming Pao* ('English with Celebrity') and *The South China Morning Post* ('On Second Thought').

For her services to Hong Kong, Her Majesty Queen Elizabeth II awarded her an Imperial Service Order in 1989 and appointed her a CBE in 1994. In 1995, she was made a JP and an Hon. Fellow of the Academy for the Performing Arts.

CYNDY WYLES was born in Wales, in the UK. That was her world until she was 18 years old, when she left for University and work. Since then she has travelled in Europe and Asia and is now based in Hong Kong. Cyndyis a mother of two children: a girl aged twenty and a boy aged seventeen, both of whom study in the UK. They all enjoy reading, theatre and classical music. Cindy first came to Hong Kong in 1997 and over the past twenty years it is the place where she has spent the greatest amount of time, although she still travels regularly between Hong Kong, Europe and the UK.

Cyndy writes, "Reading and writing bring a feeling of freedom and happiness. You can escape to, and find refuge in, the creation of a piece of fiction. I come from a nation that was described by Evelyn Waugh (in *Decline and Fall*) as having no work of artistic merit and only one talent, the ability to sing. I love poetry best because of the combined use of language, sound and rhythm."

She continues, "I have never written fiction professionally and this is the first time that I have entered a competition. I have a degree in Law but also studied Victorian Literature, and over the years I have enjoyed many Creative Writing courses in Hong Kong, UK and online."

ANTHEA YIP is 18 years old, half-Italian and half-Chinese. She lives in Hong Kong and has just completed her studies in Li Po Chun United World College.

She writes poetry and prose and is currently working on her very first novella. She has been regularly writing for school publications, a poetry club, and a literary blog. She is also a fine art student and her work explores the theme of conflict and evolution of identity.

Anthea's writing focuses on humans and their relationship to their "bubble of reality". As a writer, she recognises she must observe the world as if, "everything unfolding before her is a delicate petal slipping through the ring of her right thumb." She writes to express and to show people her inner world and the issues that matter most to her.

Anthea also performs spoken word poetry publicly to raise awareness about mental health issues. She thinks the biggest gift is being able to find beauty in the smallest of occurrences, and constantly being shocked by it, like a child.

SALLY YOUNGER is an award-winning author and science writer from Madison, Wisconsin USA. Her work has been carried by *National Geographic* and *The Saturday Evening Post*, among other outlets.

THE EDITORS

GILLIAN BICKLEY, born and educated in the United Kingdom, has lived mostly in Hong Kong since 1970. She has been a member of the Society of Authors in the United Kingdom since her school days.

Her poetry collections include *For the Record and other Poems of Hong Kong, Moving House and other Poems from Hong Kong, Sightings, China Suite, Perceptions* and the bilingual English-Romanian *Poems/Poeme*. Two collections—*Moving House* and *For the Record*—have also been published in Chinese; individual poems have been published in Arabic, Catalan, Chinese, Czech, French, German, Romanian, Turkish and other languages. *Over the Years* (2017) is a selection from her previously published work, selected by Verner Bickley. In 2014, she was awarded the "Grand Prix Orient-Occident Des Arts" at the 18th International Festival, "Curtea de Argeș Poetry Nights", held in Romania. Gillian Bickley is one of the Hong Kong poets discussed in Agnes S. L. Lam's study, *Becoming poets: The Asian English Experience*.

Gillian has written or edited several non-fiction books in different fields: *The Golden Needle: The Biography of Frederick Stewart, 1836-1889 (founder of Hong Kong Government Education)*, Hong Kong Baptist University and David C. Lam Institute for East-West Studies, 1997; *Hong Kong Invaded! A '97 Nightmare*, University of Hong Kong Press, Hong Kong, 2001; *The Development of Education in Hong Kong, 1841-1897: as revealed through the Early Education Reports of the Hong Kong Government, 1848-1896*, Proverse Hong Kong, Hong Kong, 2002; *The Stewarts of Bourtreebush*, Centre for Scottish Studies, University of Aberdeen, Scotland, 2003; *A Magistrate's Court in 19th Century Hong Kong: Court in Time*, Proverse Hong Kong, first edition, 2005; second edition, 2009; *The Complete Court Cases of Magistrate Frederick Stewart*, Proverse Hong Kong, 2008; *In Time of War* (in collaboration with Richard Collingwood-Selby), an edition based on the writings of Henry C.S. Collingwood-Selby (1898-1992), Lieutenant Commander in the Royal Navy, Proverse Hong Kong, 2013, *Through American Eyes: The Journals of George Washington (Farley) Heard (1837-1875)*, 2017; *Journeys with a Mission: Travel Journals* *of The Right Revd George Smith (1815-1871), first Bishop of Victoria, Hong Kong (1849-1865)*, Proverse Hong Kong, 2018.

Five of these fourteen English-language books received publication support from Hong Kong Arts Development Council (HKADC) and four from the Lord Wilson Heritage Trust. The extensive research necessary for seven of the non-fiction works listed was made possible by research grants awarded by the Hong Kong Baptist University and one was supported by a private sponsor.

Dr Bickley was Senior Lecturer / Associate Professor in the Department of English at the Hong Kong Baptist University for twenty-two years. She has been a full-time faculty member at the University of Lagos, Nigeria; the University of Auckland, New Zealand; and at the University of Hong Kong.

For several years, Gillian was an adjudicator at the world-famous Hong Kong Schools Music & Speech Association's annual Speech Festival and has also been a judge for the Budding Poets' Society Hong Kong.

More recently, as co-ordinator of literary activities for the English-Speaking Union Hong Kong, a non-profit registered educational charity, she has led reading appreciation sessions which are open to the community and assists to deliver reading courses at local schools. She has worked with the Gifted Education Section of the Education Bureau to encourage creative writing among students. On a freelance basis, she has taught creative reading / writing courses at the Hong Kong Academy for Gifted Education (HKAGE) and at the University of Hong Kong School for Professional and Continuing Education (HKU SPACE) and been a guest lecturer on poetry at Lingnan University Community College. Her creative reading / writing course at HKU SPACE continues to be offered. In 2016, she managed twenty and hosted seventeen meet-the-author events at a Hong Kong bookshop. On occasion, she accepts invitations to speak at school Reading Festivals and similar.

Following her career in academia, Gillian has become an experienced publisher, project-manager, text editor, and production manager, including of poetry, non-fiction, fiction and academic writing. She has been President of the Hong Kong Association of University Women and is presently a Vice-President of the Royal Asiatic Society (Hong Kong).

THE EDITORS

VERNER BICKLEY was born in the North-West of England, and educated there, in Wales and London, and has lived in Asian and Pacific countries for over fifty years.

He has been scholar, teacher, manager, broadcaster, stage and film actor and cultural diplomat in a life often enlivened by music and song, dance and entertainment.

Verner's many scholarly articles and book publications are mainly on educational and cross-cultural topics. He has however also published two volumes of memoirs: *Footfalls Echo in the Memory* and *Steps To Paradise And Beyond*. His five-book graded poetry anthology, *Poems to Enjoy*, has been popular since the 1960s. These now benefit from accompanying recordings of all poems in the texts (read mostly by himself, but some by his wife Gillian), as well as from teaching and performance notes. He is a member of the United Kingdom Society of Authors.

With his wife, Gillian, Verner Bickley is joint-publisher of Proverse Hong Kong and co-founder of the Proverse Prize and the Proverse Poetry Prize.

Verner was a naval officer in pre-independent Sri Lanka and India. He served in the Colonial Education Service in Singapore and, later, as a British Council officer in post-independence Burma, Indonesia and Japan. In Hawaii from 1971 to 1981, he served as the Director of the Culture Learning Institute at the East-West Center, established by the US Congress in Hawaii in 1960 and functioning as a US-based institution for public diplomacy with international governance, staffing, students and Fellows.

From 1972 to 1980, Verner led a small team of anthropologists, cross-cultural psychologists and linguists, focusing on the different ways in which individuals and whole societies cope in bicultural and multicultural contexts and how they address problems presented by different cultural norms. Among many interesting projects, his Institute provided for the pioneering voyage of the canoe, *Hōkūle'a*, from Hawaii to Tahiti, disproving the theories of Thor Heyerdahl.

Verner was instrumental in bringing to conferences in Honolulu writers who included Guy Amirthanayagam, Leon Edel, Vincent Eri, Nissim Ezekial, Reuel Denney, Janet Frame,

Allen Ginsberg, Syd Harrex, Thomas Keneally, Maxine Hong-Kingston, Arun Kolatkhar, Ananda Murthy, Kenzaburo Oe, Kushwant Singh, Kamala Markandaya, R.K. Narayan, A.K. Ramanajuan, E.R. Sarachchandra, Wole Soyinka and Albert Wendt.

After leaving Hawaii, and while in Saudia Arabia for a two-year assignment with the national airline, Saudia, Verner was responsible for a multi-national staff of 100 persons, mainly, but not exclusively, in Jeddah and Riyadh.

In 1983, Verner was appointed founding director of the Institute of Language in Education in Hong Kong and held that post until 1992.

Refusing to retire, Verner continues to live in Hong Kong where he writes and publishes on a variety of topics. He was founding Chairman of the English-Speaking Union (Hong Kong) and continued as Chairman of the Executive Committee for sixteen years. He recently passed this responsibility over to another person, but in his capacity as Chairman Emeritus continues with his own portfolio of tasks. As Chairman, he has traveled every year to the Mainland of China to join other judges of the national Public-Speaking Competition organised by national media. He has been an adjudicator for the Hong Kong Schools Music and Speech Association's annual Speech Festival for many years and for a while was Representative in Hong Kong for Trinity College London.

Verner Bickley's experiences have created in him an interest in cross-cultural experiences and attitudes and in a desire to communicate what he has learnt. Through his memoirs as well as his personal contacts, he hopes not only to interest others, but to encourage them to build on their own desire to learn about and empathise with other cultures.

PROVERSE HONG KONG

Together, Gillian and Verner Bickley are the publishers of Proverse Hong Kong, a Hong Kong-based press which publishes both local and international authors, including non-native speakers of English. They are also co-founders of two annual international literary prizes for work submitted in English: in 2008, they founded the Proverse Prize for unpublished book-length fiction, non-fiction or poetry, and, in 2016, they established the Proverse Poetry Prize (for single poems which may have been previously published in a language other than English). In the case of both prizes, entries are received from around the world.

Beginning in 2007 up to December 2018, Proverse has managed, edited and published about 107 English-language books by Hong Kong and international writers, five Chinese-language books and one English / Chinese bilingual book. Of the English-language books, about nineteen have been awarded publication support by Hong Kong Arts Development Council (HKADC), four by Lord Wilson Heritage Trust and one by the Ride Fund for publication in the Royal Asiatic Society Hong Kong Studies series. One received a publication grant from the Ministry of Culture of the Czech Republic and one received a publication grant from the Ministry of Culture and Tourism of the Republic of Turkey.

Twice a year, Proverse organises literary events in Hong Kong, open to the public. New books are launched, writers are introduced and launching authors give brief talks. Announcements are made relating to the current year's Proverse Prize and Proverse Poetry Prize and prizes are presented to those authors who are present.

Gillian and Verner work hard to bring authors before the reading public. In 2016, they arranged twenty meet-the-author sessions, held at a Hong Kong bookshop. Edited videos of these talks are available on Youtube.

Of the titles published by Proverse, several have attracted a Preface or advance appreciation from figures of international reputation, most notably perhaps, from Václav Havel (for the English translation of Olga Walló's *Tightrope: A Bohemian Tale*).

Two titles (Peter Gregoire's, *Article 109* and *The Devil You Know*) were best sellers at Dymocks Hong Kong.

The publication by Proverse of the late Sophronia Liu's book, *A Shimmering Sea*, was a major argument in the award to Sophronia of a posthumous PhD at the University of Minnesota.

Other writers published by Proverse have also benefited in their literary careers.

Gillian's and Verner's own books and all those by other authors published by Proverse, are available internationally as well as locally, including through the Chinese University of Hong Kong Press. There are copies in the British Library and other legal deposit libraries in the United Kingdom, the Hong Kong Public Library system, as well as in many university and public libraries world-wide.

POETS' NOTES AND COMMENTARIES

[1] Joy Al-Sofi tells us that writing on geology is not something she has done before. She continues, "Our earth is a blue planet and was once even more so, a place where water was everywhere—almost everywhere. One of the very few places existing above water then is the Kalahari Craton of southern Africa, around which Gondwana, the most ancient of continents, formed.

"For some of us, we get it, our earth is precious. But some humans are actively in the process of destroying all life, including our own. Most seem oblivious or simply can't be bothered.

"In Namibia, you can see the varied landscapes evincing the tectonic and volcanic convulsions. Many of the most ancient rocks have gone through many eons of weathering and erosion, carried to the sea, blown back to land again. This process was repeated many times and currently forms the great sand dunes of the Namib desert.

"For the most part, all landscapes are old, but I felt very moved by these most ancient of exposed and often harsh landscapes, knowing they existed, were shaped, created, and destroyed long before the presence of human life on this planet. They began in a realm beyond our comprehension, and it seems they are the original cradle from which we sprang. From cradles to mothers. I wanted to see if I could, through poetry, touch in others what Earth's geology touched in me."

[2] Of her poem, 'In the Presence', Joy Al-Sofi writes, "It's always great to find a new passion. In the past few years, I have fallen in love with seeing wildlife in their natural habitats. Close encounters with elephants are among the most splendid experiences you can have.

"One of the most counter-intuitive aspects of elephants, the largest land mammal, is how they don't thunder through the bush, nor set the earth to shaking with their every step. They are absolute stealth. But that's not the only surprise, when they go behind a small amount of bush they can completely disappear, or nearly so.

"I wanted to share my admiration for, and concerns about, these special animals that are threatened by human actions. I was eager to address this issue, especially, here in Hong Kong where the sale of ivory is still legal, under the pretense of selling 'old' ivory stocks. This market means increased poaching of elephants for their tusks, which cannot be removed without the death or butchering of the animal.

"This poem is a way of conveying my respects to elephants through the imperfect medium of human language, which can create distance even as it seeks to make connections. And the finest means of expression in language is poetry."

[3] Indran Armithanayagam wrote, 'Nice', "thinking of Baltimore and Edgar Allen Poe, who breathed his last on a streetcorner in that grimy, port city. I was thinking too of bangers and mash, a favorite food of my English sojourn. As Cavafy wrote, you carry your city with you wherever you go. I carry my loves, hence Poe, bangers and mash into this poem."

[4] Thea Biesheuvel tells us this about her poem, 'Reformation'.
"This poem is about my mother, (Maria Bertha van Bruggen-Biesheuvel).

"Writing about one's mother is, for most, quite difficult. The view in close-up is very different to the view from outside the immediate family. My mother was also a complex woman and we were often at odds. As I aged, I understood her better. Her change from mainstay of our family with close relations with her siblings was suddenly disrupted when they decided to emigrate from The Netherlands to Australia (in 1953). We all had to make major adjustments, in language, in cultural practices and in attitude.

"My family (name) and history is relatively well-known in The Netherlands, but in Australia we were just another 'strange' family, with odd clothes and accents.

"Despite this, her kids (me included), did adapt. Her grandchildren are no different from the general population. Her great-grandchildren hardly know the family's origins. This pained my mother a great deal.

"The poem's inspiration comes from, 'The Reformation Hymn', associated with the breakaway Protestant religion (from the Roman Catholic faith), and starts with the line, 'ein feste burg ist unsere Gott' (a mighty fortress is Our Lord), and my poem follows its rhythms.

"My mother was that mighty fortress for a long time and I'm sad that she had such a hard time adapting to the loss of all she had prior to our migration.

"A specific phrase 'a lekker koekie' was her chief delight, in that it was a 'very tasty biscuit or cake' which she looked forward to every afternoon. She died in 1996 aged 92."

[5] Maria Elena Blanco has given the following interesting accounts of the inspiration for each of her poems.

'Axis of silence'
"A poem about communication and emotional intelligence in relationships, and the lack thereof. Many associations arise, among them a reference to a book turned into film, *The Silence of the Lambs*."

'Nightbirds'
"Three poets on a night out at a New York Lower East Side bar with that name, what New Yorkers would call a bit snobbishly 'a hole in the wall'. Two are working on well-advanced projects, the other one is eagerly starting out and basks ecstatically in the dark glow of wine and lived-in poetry. The dawn will bring a poem."

'On reading Baudelaire after a Poet's burial'
"This poem was written in memory of the Austrian poet Gerhard Kofler, deceased in 2005, whom I translated into Spanish (from German/Italian) and who was a dear friend. At his burial, as we were reaching his burial site and prayers were being said, the weather suddenly turned quite stormy, a very dark cloud appeared, it started hailing, it got extremely cold and humid... This left a strong impression on me. He was a fond reader of Baudelaire and the other French 19th century poets, I was in the middle of a Baudelaire translation at the time and travelling the next day, taking that work with me. All these associations mingled in my mind to produce this poem."

'Rambling digression at Thomas Bernhard's grave'
"A visit to the great Austrian writer's grave after much walking around trying to find it at Grinzing cemetery. No signs, no maps, no clues of any kind. I finally had to go searching for someone who could possibly tell me where it was. It was in a very accessible part of the grounds but almost totally covered by ivy and did not show the writer's name but that of his lady friend's, hospital companion's, putative life partner's, whom he met at a sanatorium while being treated for TB. Once there, all kinds of associations from his autobiography, which I had recently read, and from some of his novels and plays, cropped up, to be later intermingled in the poem. The shape of the poem suggests a partial side view of the baroque cross that adorned the grave."

'Rich Jain temple, Mumbai'
"This poem, written after my trip to India, was inspired by a visit to a Jain temple as I watched the faithful go about their rites and prayers, which were totally new to me, and as I subsequently read a bit about this religion, which I then found fascinating, especially from a philosophical point of view. It was also inevitable that I try to see myself from outside myself—that is, poetically—against that background and reflect on how diversity impacts one's consciousness. In that process, unconscious effects also surface in the images and words of the poem."

'White-gloved poetess'
"The poem is in memory of Austrian poet Heidi Pataki, who died in 2006 and some of whose poetry I translated into Spanish. It refers to a bilingual reading in which we both read those poems, her offer of payment for the translations—a kind of barter against a pair of gold earrings that had been her Grandmother's. A very elegant gesture on her part and somehow a very Viennese one. Little did we know then that she would not live much longer, as the rumours about her sudden and fatal illness would soon suggest."

'Writing out of no place'
"Being too sick to keep a date to carry out a poetic exercise at a church makes the writer become out of sync with time and space and create a poem with associations drawn from church-related events in her life which are then transposed into the poem in a seemingly virtual time and space, the time and space of writing."

[6] Paola Caronni explains that her poem, 'The Terrarium', "highlights the powerful and destructive force of words in important relationships. Grief and helplessness emerge once the values of a long-time friendship and the unique connection of two souls are lost. The glass terrarium was once a special and private environment, where this friendship could thrive without the need for any external nourishment or stimulus, but just through mutual respect and understanding."

[7] Josie Chambers explains that the poem, 'Cell', looks at the way in which we all, perhaps women especially, build for ourselves small prisons. Blake in his poem 'London' calls these prisons "mind-forged manacles." The poem explores the idea that some kind of "mind-forged" escape is always possible.

[8] Lauriane Chappé tells us that she wrote, 'Facing the Sea', in 2016 at a time when she wanted to leave the Paris region, find a new place of residence and, in a way, start a new life. She continues, "We need to understand the word 'country' in terms of 'region'. Indeed, it is in my native region, the French Riviera, more precisely in Nice, that I found an appeasement. As I was watching the waves of the Mediterranean sea, it seemed obvious to me that this place, where I come from but where I have never lived, was suddenly here for me, at this particular moment of my life. Is it a simple bracket in my life or permanent anchorage, I do not know yet, but settling down here has definitely silenced for a time my other needs and thoughts. My hesitations and my desire to explore more places vanished and gave way to the simple serenity of the present time. Today I feel good and I know that here I found a place where I will always be able to be fulfilled."

⁹ Lauriane Chappé tells us that her poem, 'Wandering Feelings', was written in 2017, about an afternoon that she spent in the countryside, in the mountains of Southern France. "I was visiting my godfather. His brother and some neighbours were there also. My parents had passed away a few years before, so these people are basically what is remaining of my family and with whom I share my roots. I was happy to leave the hectic life of the city to visit them in a chalet in the middle of nature. My godfather is a good cook and he prepared delicious local meals for the occasion. After lunch, I felt the need to go for a walk around this beautiful place, while the rest of my family had gone for a nap. I lost track of time and eventually fell asleep in nature, perhaps because of the lavish meal and the feeling of tipsiness as well. The simple fact of being waited for, of knowing that after my walk I would find a warm and welcoming place, made my get-away even more delightful. That day, I felt I was in perfect harmony with both nature and my hosts."

¹⁰ Neil Douglas explains that his poem, 'Empathy for the Devil', is a different take on the Doctor/Patient relationship and comes from his experience working as a family doctor in the UK.

¹¹ As for his three poems, 'The transient intimacy of London Transport', 'The Imposition of Ashes', and 'Amor Vincit Omnium' (Love Conquers all), Neil Douglas comments, "Although different in style [they] can be read as a triptych on the theme of Love. The first is fantasised and unrequited. The second perhaps requited but nevertheless made transient by Life and Death. The third is Love endured but enduring."

¹² Hasan Erkek tells the story of his poem, 'Mermaid'.
"I was born in the mountain village of Uzunköy, in Adıyaman, in the east of Anatoila. Then the family moved to the small town of Doğanşehir, where I spent most of my childhood. I started to write poetry there when I was aged nine. When I was a student at secondary school my teachers published my first poetry book.

"When I was fourteen, I went to the small city of Tekirdağ, for my high school studies. Three years later I went to Ankara to study at university. Five years after that, I was employed by Anadolu University in Eskişehir, a city near Istanbul.

"By then, I was really tired of always moving from one place to another, feeling like an immigrant.

"When I went to Eskişehir I was twenty-four. I didn't want to move around anymore.

"I met a young girl there. She was from İstanbul, from the seaside. She looked like a Mermaid. So I called her, "Mermaid". She signed her notes, her letters to me, "Mermaid". And I wrote this poem for her. But she had to return to İstanbul, to her family.

"She never knew I had written this poem..."

Hasan Erkek explains that the word, "kharamees", means, "gangster", and refers to the word as used in the, "well-known oriental folk tale, 'Ali Baba and 40 Kharamees', or, 'Ali Baba and the Forty Thieves'."

[13] Hilary Faulkner writes, "The poem, 'A Mother's Love', was written with deep passion about the emotions evoked by living with a chronic disease, and how, without her mother's support, she would most definitely not be in such good shape both mentally and physically. It was written from the heart about the strong bond she has with her mum. She has now almost reached remission which she in some part puts down to the absolute love and strength from her mother."

[14] D. J. Hamilton gives the following notes about his poems.

'The Hummingbird Sometimes Flies Backwards'
"I was re-examining Imagism and the role of imagery in my own work. This poem emerged from an assignment in a workshop at the Port Townsend Writer's Conference led by the great Chinese-American poet, Arthur Sze."

'The Giant'
"This is a poem in the form of a parable. Tyrants often evoke family or blood relationship to manipulate the masses and mask abuses of power."

'Why Are There Actors?'
"The death of the brilliant actor Phillip Seymour Hoffman affected me deeply. Much later, while revising the poem, the death of Robin Williams hit me like the second half of a 1-2 punch."

'After'
"I was in a long-distance relationship with a partner in another country and our lives were going in different directions. The poem is written from the partner's point of view."

[15] Stephen Herman writes, "'Pilgrim of the Screen' was inspired by a 17th century rosewood screen with mirrors and images of the gods painted on the back of glass. The screen was brought from China in the late 1800s and is on a wall in my living-room. We are all pilgrims making our way to the Happiness Isle, just like the images on the glass inserts."

[16] Antony Huen writes this about his poem, 'Dear J: In the Banyan Forest'.
"I have been writing a series of poems addressing a mysterious, non-unitary figure called 'J', and the poem which appears here in the anthology is based on a digital image of a landscape painting by the Chinese painter Deng Fen (1894-1964). In the painting, two men are playing different Chinese musical instruments in the middle of a forest."

[17] Christos Koukis writes about his poem, 'The ugly side of History'.
"I am a poet from Greece, a country with a great history on the crossroads of East and West, on the crossroads of time, a country that throughout centuries has been influenced by many cultures and civilizations. Living nowadays in Greece I face every day the huge number of war and economic refugees from the Middle East and the Eastern world generally, the

conservative ideas and prejudices that still exist and oppress, and the ugly face of Western capitalism.

"I wrote this poem to express my thoughts, my strong beliefs and my protest on behalf of all these people who don't have a voice and barely have a future. It's a request for justice for all underprivileged men and women around the world and a product of my consciousness that living as a poet in a free country I have a duty to all the rest who are not lucky enough to be on the good side of history.

"The poem contains everyday stories about people I have met in the city where I live: people who lost their jobs because of the financial crisis and have to live on the street, people who left their countries because of war, people who are victims of racism because they are homosexuals, people who failed to achieve the western dream and have become addicts out on the fringe—and many more stories. These people are my inspiration. For these people I am writing this poem and these are the people I want to speak up for."

[18] Carol Krauss explains that her poem, 'Barefoot', is a simple reflection of her childhood, and the neighborhood she grew up in many, many years ago in South Carolina. It was one of the poems she wrote during National Poetry Month.

[19] Lynda Lambert explains that her intention in writing her poem, 'Flying Off to Wales' (in 2018), was to write a "letter" poem. "I wrote it in the form of a letter, or an E-mail message. This poem was created from an E-mail communication with my friend and colleague, Dr Ann Paton.

"Ann is a retired college Professor of English, and an Episcopal Priest. She spends time every year at St David's Wales and she wrote to tell me about a forthcoming trip in the summer of 2018. I combined her actual words in the E-mail, with my own thoughts about her trip. This poem grew from that dialogue with Dr Ann. The poem is a 'found poem', in which I used the actual E-mail conversation between us."

[20] Of her poem, 'Yes I Sing', written in 2017-18, Lynda says, "I was writing a great deal of ABECEDARIAN poems for over a year. I was trying to write one for every letter of the alphabet—26 in total. This poem is in the ABECEDARIAN FORM. The first word of each line is in alphabetical order, beginning with A, and ending with Z.

"I was thinking about my favorite words when I started writing this poem. I listed those words first. Then, I expanded my idea to place those words in the context and variety of techniques found in and explored in the writing of a Post-Modern Poem. I explore ideas about time and memory and my own preference for some of my favourite words."

[21] Susan Lavender writes about her poem, 'Consumed'.
"This poem is about my love-hate relationship with Italy. Being half-English and half-Italian by birth, I was born with something of a split personality due to the diametrically opposed cultural influences of my two countries. I loved Italy immensely as a child and growing up as a teenager. I became very disillusioned by it later in life, however, through the suffering and distress caused to my mother and myself in her last years and at the time of her death, due, among other things, to a relentless, unforgiving bureaucracy.

"Making the disillusionment more painful is the fact that my love for Italy still underlies and pervades my negative feelings, as highlighted in a humorous tone in this poem by one aspect of its culture that I will always cherish."

[22] Susan Lavender writes that her poem, 'Fowl and Feline', is about her pre-Handover days living in Hong Kong's Discovery Bay. "It was inspired by local artist Lorette Roberts's painting of the Edward Lear poem 'The Owl and the Pussycat', in which the boat was a little Chinese sampan bobbing around in Hong Kong's Victoria Harbour!

"I took the 7.20 ferry each morning to go to work at UNHCR (the United Nations Refugee Agency) in Hong Kong, where I did refugee status determination reports on Vietnamese asylum-seekers. A middle-aged English man and woman regularly took the 7.20 ferry but they were no ordinary married couple. In fact theirs was just a platonic relationship, doomed to fail. 1997 was soon to separate them in different directions. Like the Owl and the Pussycat, this couple shared a particular type of homeless desperation and a pipe-dream of escaping together to something better yet unattainable. They symbolise the fragile status of people who had come to Hong Kong on a temporary work basis but for whom it had gradually become home. Some had burnt their boats and had nothing to return to in their own countries by the time 1997's tidal wave ended the particular type of work they did, such as working with the Vietnamese asylum-seekers.

"The poem therefore has two themes. First, it deals with what happens when you unwittingly build your life on a raft at sea rather than on solid land, that is, developing a permanent dependence on a temporary person or place. Secondly, it reflects the fact that relationships are seldom what they outwardly appear to be and those who are psychologically compatible may not end up together for purely practical reasons, such as being of different species."

[23] Jemima Law explains that 'Lies' was written after the first time she experienced heartbreak. "As I was young and didn't know any better, I felt angry, confused and betrayed—and directed all that energy into my poem. Although short, it is inspired by how I missed all the signs that he was never the right person for me; dishonest, manipulative and selfish. Yet, I still chose to stay with him because I was scared to let go. Feeling torn between my head and my heart, my heart won every time, for better or for worse."

[24] Elbert Siu Ping Lee explains that his poem, 'Your Refuge', written in the Twin Cinema format, is meant to be read in two different ways.

"One can read each stanza column by column and then read verses across the columns. The arrangement allows for an exploration of feminine power by juxtaposing the meanings of refuge and love.

"Reading the first stanza, column by column, the verses 'your refuge, an ever-expanding physical space' begin to raise issues with what we generally understand as refuge-seeking. If refuge is about protection and sustenance, then love, and perhaps desire too, always accompany it. In the folktale of Cinderella, a poor peasant girl with an abusive stepmother finds her prince and love, and 'ascends' to life in a palace—her refuge.

"To some, this story is 'gender-tainted'. To others, it reflects a human norm. Exchanging love and/or sex for refuge occurs not only in legends but is alive and well in present-day Hong Kong—the metropolis known for equating love with apartment ownership for many women.

"Refuge-seeking in the context of love is further explored in the first stanza when it is read across the columns—'your refuge, an eight headed gargoyle in nascence...' This brings into focus the relationship between refuge and the dark triad of security, control, and power—a core part of the female psyche without which, it is said, desire and love are not possible.

"In the Chinese love story, Qixi, however, gender power distribution as commonly perceived is reversed. Unlike Cinderella who 'ascends' to high places in her love, the heroine Weaver, a young goddess of the skies, abandons her privileged 'career' of rainbow making and 'descends' from heaven to live with a poor Cowherd. A sense of this female-initiated love is portrayed in the column by column reading of the second stanza.

"However, the female psyche can do more, she may possess love powers that are hidden, from a 'higher plane'; she does not simply stop at material exchange. This particular form of feminine power is described in the across-columns reading of the second stanza, 'an eight faced goddess seeking alliance, my refuge, at harrowing times, turning into contours of undulating presence...'. This shift of awareness of love and sex on the part of women frees them from socio-economic and cultural trappings. They are now powerful, self-reliant, and therefore capable of 'descending' deeper into life.

"The enlightened female psyche, instead of seeking refuge in 'an ever expanding physical space' and 'climate control' as described in the first stanza, now envisions herself and her body as a sacred space. She is now the high priestess and the lead goddess, and her body, a true temple with a climate of her own, is set to unveil the original face of sex and love—'your body, evolving sacred space.' This primal form of 'love-power' is captured in the last few lines of the second stanza 'you banned the climate control, therefore tomorrow is not promised, upsetting the pillows, what are now vacant—a feast unstoppable—faith.'"

Elbert provides the following Notes.
"1. The Twin Cinema format in poetry was introduced by the Singaporean poet Yeow Kai Chai. Related forms of textual composition in which verses can be connected in various ways are exemplified in the works of the Antiguan-Canadian poet Tanya Evanson. In her book *Bothism*, it is suggested that these forms of writing can be found in ancient Sufi texts and Chinese poetry. More recent poetic work adopting the Twin Cinema format can be found in *Twin Cities: An anthology of twin cinema from Singapore and Hong Kong* edited by Joshua Ip and Tammy Ho Lai-Ming.
"2. In Buddhist taxonomy, the number eight is associated with perfection. The circle is described as four sides and eight directions. In Tibetan buddhism, the saint Padmasambhava is said to have eight manifestations and has been translated into 八面玲瓏 in Chinese or 'eight skilful personalities.' Other Buddhist contexts speak of the eight guardian gods and spirits. The term first appeared as Sanskrit, and later in Chinese as 天龍八部. The Chinese term is better known as the title of the novel by Cha Jin-yong.
"3. Female mythological figures as refuge providers and goddesses of primal love are prominent in Greek and Iranian legends. Persephone 'descends' into the underworld to bond with the hidden and mysterious Hades. Ishtar, a goddess herself, braves hell to save her unworthy shepherd lover Dumuzid. It is interesting to note that the interpretations of these myths can go both ways. While it may be said that these are fantasies of past and present patriarchies, it can also be argued that these fantasies undermine the patriarchies in which they were formed."

[25] Ho Cheung LEE (Peter) explains the background to his poem, 'Receptionist', as follows. "My paternal grandmother's funeral was held in the morning of 3 April 2018. Everyone

seemed to have a duty and I was given a role at the reception desk outside the hall. I sat there alone, waiting, looking at Grandma's smiling photo and appreciating her as a role model. No words could express my sorrow at that moment. I composed this verse shortly after the ceremony."

[26] Selena Liang writes about her poem 'Sound Refugee'. "I listen to my mundane reality in the Mass Transit Railway of Hong Kong. It usually takes an hour to reach the university, but fifteen minutes is enough to spark the urge to plug my earphones into the vacuum. I think of my wasted time, my fading existence—a similar feeling is romanticised in Alan Walker's masterpiece, 'Faded'. I think of Hong Kong, which is often likened to a sea-wet rock in colonial-period literature. I think of the Cantopop playlist—once a symbol of Hong Kong glory but now I seldom play from it. I think about the classical hero fading into the ordinary. I listen to Hong Kong songwriter Albert Leung's 'King of Karaoke' （K歌之王）, which tells the story of a boy singing innumerable romantic songs in karaoke sessions, but unable to win the heart of his crush. The music industry is chained in futile production, so are Hong Kong and myself. The song tells of the failure to inspire love; but is itself inspiring."

[27] J. P. Linstroth explains that his poem, 'The Crossing', is about migrants coming from Central America and Mexico to the US borderlands.

[28] Jack Mayer writes about his three poems as follows.

'Blood'
"For most of my career I have been a primary care pediatrician. I began practicing in a very rural area of northern Vermont, on the Canadian border, in a town with the lowest income in the state of Vermont. Mine was the first pediatric practice in Eastern Franklin County and the need was great. I began writing poems about my patients as a way of understanding and empathizing with the challenges of their lives. 'Blood' is inspired by a house call I made during a snowstorm to a very poor family living in a trailer on Troy Street."

'Psalm 23/Hospice Volunteer'
"I am a Hospice volunteer and singer in our local Hospice singing group. Our small group sings at the bedside for those nearing the end of life and their families. This poem is a tribute to the volunteers who minister to the dying with their unconditional presence and love. Their generosity of time and spirit is what I experience as holiness and grace made plain."

'The God Particle'
"I am fascinated by the intersection of metaphysics and particle physics. When I heard of the 4 July 2012 discovery of the Higgs boson, a long sought fundamental particle of nature, often referred to as the 'God Particle', I was inspired to write this poem. The Higgs boson particle was detected at the Large Hadron Collider, the most powerful particle accelerator in the world. Finding the Higgs boson proved the existence of the invisible "Higgs Field" that confers mass onto everything we know by giving mass to elementary particles such as electrons and protons.
"'In the beginning was the Higgs Field....'"

[29] Rony Nair explains that his poem, 'An Actress Dies at a Wedding' refers to the sad, accidental death of the Indian film star Sridevi in February 2018, and uses it, "as a staging point to talk about index points of incidental memory and entwined association. There are references to specific benchmarks and their recollections in one's memory of shared pasts; and permanent divergence."

Of his poem, 'Carp', Rony Nair says, "It is a take on dogma and organised religion and its association with the rules of the head. Rhetoric and hearsay overruling the prescient. The original intent, where there was one, is lost in the equivocations of human folly and fanfaronade."

[30] As background to her poem, 'Emotional Refugee', N. Noéll writes, "I have lived in five countries and five different states within the United States of America as a result of family business and spouse relocation. Each time I moved to a new place, I left behind friends and things that I loved. I then had to

assimilate quickly to a new environment and make new friends. Despite each move resulting in better opportunities, I had to search for security and stability. My parents taught me to work hard but hard work is not always sufficient. I owe it to many people for my academic and personal achievement. I would not want to be a refugee. But the day I stepped onto this promised land, I was already a refugee of sorts."

[31] Keith Nunes explains that his poem, 'You can have my seat', deals with a sense of estrangement within a close relationship that has become unworkable for one party. The sense that the strong attachment may be weakening but for a long while breaking it seems impossible, then an epiphany occurs—a moment when you realise it is possible and the accompanying sense of freedom is overwhelmingly positive.

[32] Patience O'Neill's poem, 'Catalonia', was inspired by the work of Gaudi and the city of Barcelona. "I took a trip to Barcelona, a city in the province of Catalonia, Spain. People from Catalonia feel they are in a separate social and political group from the rest of Spain. Catalonians are famous for their energy and creativity. Gaudi the architect, who lived in Barcelona, is famous for his original, mould-breaking architectural designs." Patience describes her poem as "a haibun", the last three lines being in the form of a haiku.

[33] Danny Poon writes this of his poem, 'Not Forgotten'. "The suppressed is the name of women; to suppress is the name of men. From time to time, a number of women have tried to live a life of their own, but then they became confined. However, their free spirits have kept our hope alive. This poem is written as a tribute to all these women, including my mother, who all fought this battle well. Your legacies live on."

[34] Of her poem, 'Amber', Rochelle Potkar writes, "Sometimes when we go in search of a past love, the world might rake up much more than a simple answer to what once was. It might open a library of travesties that reflect personal agonies. This poem was an attempt at sketching that."

³⁵ As translated by Natalie Nera, Simona Rackova has this to say about her poem, 'Hair by Hair': "What is poetry to me? In our rationally organised world, it represents search for the openings that lead to the original state of chaos; to the moment when Time flows like lava, when everything is fluid, uncertain and incomplete. Is it the scrunched up pieces of paper on the bottom of one's school bag or snow balls? From my memories, I extract skeletons of the fish my Dad used to catch and I, my hands trembling, would bring them to my mum in the cottage above the river. And my loves: the one that passed comes back again without warning. I love anything that occurs suddenly when we start dreaming. Or writing."

³⁶ Joanna Radwańska-Williams writes that, at the time of writing her poem, 'Dreams of Evening', she was living in Macau in a flat overlooking the schoolyard of Anglican College. "Every morning, the cheerful voices of children playing outside mixed with the chirping of birds in the trees. The children's world is carefree, but the adult world is constraining. When I wake up, as an adult, I realize that the day will constrain my freedom. I wish that I could sleep again, and be transformed into a carefree butterfly.

"The poem also contains wordplay of the similar-sounding words 'caterpillar' (the precursor of a butterfly) and 'capillaries' (small blood vessels, which when full of blood, help the newly-hatched butterfly to stretch its wings). The blood of a butterfly is called hemolymph, and is different from human blood, but I used the word 'blood' in the poem."

³⁷ Joanna Radwańska-Williams explains the background to her poem, 'The Tartness of Unknowing' as follows. "Once my Fulbright English Teaching Assistant, John He, told me that his thirst for knowledge was driven by his never-ending sense of unsatisfied curiosity. Being a young man, he was surprised when I told him this feeling of insatiety never goes away. This led me to reminisce about my own quest for knowledge. For example, when I was researching my Ph.D. dissertation, a nineteenth-century German journal I had requested from the library came to me covered in copious layers of dust. I felt very grateful to the librarian who had ordered it generations ago, and

equally grateful to subsequent generations of librarians, the custodians of knowledge, who had not thrown it away! Also, in the poem, 'the well inside my mind' refers to intuitive (some would say, inborn) knowledge. This is the well inside which I sometimes catch poems, like fish."

[38] Patrick T. Reardon writes about his poem 'Buttons'.
"In the odd way of art, the spark for this poem was a love song by the French singer Zazie titled, 'Femmes Tefales'. The song is in French except for the word, 'tefales', which is Spanish. It means 'Teflon'. In the song, the singer's lover is distracted by his Teflon women, at least, that's what the Google translation seems to say. 'Teflon women', for me, brought to mind all those very rich, perfectly-dressed women in fashion magazines who seem impervious to anything negative. Putting them on the page led to their men and the buttons they push to accomplish things and their perfect lawns…and the guy who cares for their lawn and has his own life, unknown to them."

[39] Melissa Ann Reed writes about her poem, 'Listening to Chang'e read on Mid-Autumn Moon Festival'.
"After flying to the moon, Chinese myth's Chang'e reads to Japanese myth's Hime, also flown to the moon to prevent her from becoming a child-bride. Their meeting at the Chinese Mid-Autumn Moon Festival represents reunion and wholeness from that which has separated them—too much masculine energy called 'yang'. As such, their reunion 'puts the lid on yang' so that yin or feminine energy may increase for the regeneration of life. 'Wen Lin' refers to both a forest of characters or ideograms and a forest of literary personae. For Chinese, the past is before them; the future is behind, such that the unknown or mystery of life becomes regenerative of humility and the open-mindedness needed for discovery learning. The poem echoes Agnes de Mille's advice to her dancers."

[40] Melissa Ann Reed explains that her poem 'Mid-Autumn Moon Festival, Lake Harriet, Linden Hills', "celebrates the Chinese harvest and reunion festival near a Minnesota lake in the Linden Hills neighbourhood of Minneapolis, named after

the Native American Minnehaha, bride of Hiawatha, whose ancestors crossed the Bering Straits from China. Lake Harriet implicitly calls to my mind the delightful Harriet Harlan, daughter and granddaughter of the two Supreme Court Harlan Judges who stood for African American equal rights."

[41] Melissa Ann Reed's poem, 'White Clouds, Red Trees' envisions the Chinese Ninth Chrysanthemum Moon Festival of early November.

[42] Vinni Relwani explains that she wrote the poem, 'Signals', many years ago, during and after the onset of a physical health issue. Writing was a form of expression that proved to be cathartic for her. This poem has taken on additional meaning at present, as someone close to her is going through their own challenges now. The poem has resurfaced to her mind, as a vessel of hope and encouragement for that person too.

[43] Angelo Rizzi tells us this about his three poems.
"I wrote these three poems five years ago, all at the same period. It was one of the worst periods of my life from an emotional point of view.

"As a consequence, I produced an abundant and interesting poetic work:—ninety-three poems in two and a half years.

"Poetry has saved my life! At least metaphorically. Deep inside I know I have saved myself by searching for a solution in the labyrinth of my experiences.

"The fundamental issue linking, 'Homo erectus', 'I count the inert hours', and, 'The notebook', is *hope*. Hope springs eternal!—Hope announcing a change, which actually happened...."

[44] Halil Suat Saraç explains that his poem, 'Driving My Lips to the Rainclouds', is an attempt to depict a love relationship. "In this poem", he writes, "the woman's body is not conceived as a soft instrument of the mind, but rather a rough and textured reality of the earth. Through his lover's reality, the speaker of the poem digests the universe and finds joy in his struggle within it."

⁴⁵ Sanja Särman gives us the following notes about her four poems.

'Schoolyard Memories' is about children's games.

'The Burier of Flowers Lamenting' is inspired by Lin Daiyu's poem about Burying Falling Petals (葬花吟) from Cao Xueqin's eighteenth century classic, *The Dream of The Red Chamber*.

'The Fog' is inspired by the almost impenetrable fog that rolled in from the sea one day when she lived in Hong Kong.

'The Only Thing' is inspired in part by and devoted entirely to the persona of the Japanese writer Yukio Mishima.

⁴⁶ Allegra Silberstein tells us that she wrote, 'A Grace of Light', "remembering a time when I was young and sad. Always then I would go for a walk in the woods to find solace there and one magical afternoon this miracle happened for me that has stayed with me all my life."

⁴⁷ Writing of her villanelle, 'Let this refuge sing!', Hayley Ann Solomon first comments on the villanelle structure ("a nineteen-line poetic form consisting of five tercets followed by a quatrain"). Of her own poem, she writes, "You might notice there are two refrains and two repeating rhymes, with the first and third line of the first tercet repeated alternately until the last stanza, which includes both repeated lines." She tells us that she chose the villanelle form because she considered its musicality to be, "almost an echo of birdsong, the thematic texture of this poem".

⁴⁸ Of, 'My refuge for a while!', Hayley Ann Solomon writes, "There are so many different kinds of refuge. In this poem, I wanted to depict refuge as a place of the heart, a haven of the soul and an exuberance of spirit. I chose iambic rhythm for its soothing cadence yet coupled this with a structure of alternating tetrameter and trimeter to generate excitement. The

recurring rhyme scheme abab cccb adds a degree of quirkiness that reflects the unexpected nature of the refuge, and yet its predestined, almost predictable nature by the poem's end."

[49] Hayley Ann Solomon explains that, 'There never was nothing', is a free-form poem imbued with elements of kiwiana, images and cosmology indigenous to New Zealand. "I rely heavily here on sound play, assonance, consonance, alliteration and the convergence of opposites. I end on my ultimate conclusion; moments matter. Beautiful moments, forged by nature, patience, time and the recognition of beauty, become an ultimate refuge."

[50] Of her poem, 'Abandoned Beauty', Luisa Ternau explains, "Feelings are fleeting, for the majority of people at least. In the poem, a young girl has become a teenager. Her most recent stage in life comes with new interests which overpower all things from the past, even those full of beauty. The doll, almost personified, is shown in her total ignorance of events. Her beauty is now neglected by the person who loved her most, and by all her surroundings. And yet, she shows hope in the face of neglect."

[51] Luisa Ternau explains that, in her poem, 'For So Sweet is the Sound of My Lute', "Reminiscences of a real geisha's interview are interwoven with a European medieval fantasy, involving a beggar turned into a famous lute player, who is musing here on the perception of individuals' roles in society and on the price that the pursuit of artistic creativity takes."

[52] Luisa Ternau's poem, 'Seller of Dreams', "features a dialogue between a seller of dreams and his potential customer. In the end, the seller shows how obsessive the role of dreams is in life."

[53] Edward Tiesse writes about his poem, 'Tuscan Autumn'. "In October 2017 I was hiking in Tuscany and it had not rained all summer. The land was parched and as I walked, my footsteps echoed each other and sounded to me like ghostly whispers.

The land and the region's history melded and I thought of their influence on art and literature."

[54] Roger Uren writes that his poem, 'The Failure of Typhoons', "was inspired by the contrast between Typhoon Mangkut, which did much physical damage to Hong Kong, and the ego-dominated political dynamics that seem to be becoming more common, and are leading to policies based on the motive of promoting one's own image and status, rather than making the world a better and safer place."

[55] Peter Verbica writes, "An author's explanation at times removes some of the romanticism and mystery of a piece, a bit like a friend who tells you the ending of a good movie that you've been wanting to see. It can interrupt a reader's reverie. But, since the editors request a 'backstory', I will give one.

"If the poem 'Stain', is a success, you will discern my goals: to, as Yeats writes, 'cast a cold eye;' to be honest, despite the inelegance; to chronicle the death of a marriage—with its devastating aftermath; to be efficient with one's words; and to have thematic cohesion.

"I could tell you more of the sentimental details; how my family and I lived in a rambling Monterey Colonial which overlooked the ocean; how my youngest of four daughters locked herself in the bathroom and screamed uncontrollably about wanting to kill herself when she heard the news of her parents' impending divorce; how I listened to her logic of why she thought she would die young because that is what sad people do; of the lawn being left unwatered and more.

"Instead, years after the event, where time may heal the wound, but the scar is still evident if you unbutton the shirt, I wrote a brief poem and called it, 'Stain.'"

[56] Writing of his poem, 'Magic Hell', David Vognar explains that he works as a social worker and has seen addiction's allure and destruction up close, as well as recovery from addiction.

[57] Olga Walló writes, "I am seventy now, my friend is eighty-six. My last collection of poems (in my mother-tongue, Czech) is entitled, Love in Later Life. This poem belongs to the way

we live together. My message: Dear People, don't be afraid to become old... and older. It is an interesting process... thrilling... full of change... of developing emotions.... Be brave enough to enjoy it."

[58] Bruce Arlen Wasserman's, '8 Months in Warsaw' is, "an attempt to step inside the universality of the human condition when displacement by force of war overtakes the expected rhythms within a calendar of daily living. The poem was inspired by my own family's experiences at the onset of World War II: my grandfather escaping a call-up as a Polish Army Reservist—leaving his family behind for what was expected to be a short conflict, something easily resolved by Poland's self-perceived military might. Impossible to imagine was the Holocaust that followed the Nazis' rapid conquest of the Polish State and the segregation and destruction of Poland's Jewish population. Once thus oppressed, my family's experience in Warsaw became a struggle for daily survival that removed the quotient of dreams from everyday life. I have written this poem in the narrative voice of my mother, who was fourteen years old at the onset of the Holocaust."

[59] Richard Westley explains that the title of his poem, 'Obliquy', is a play on the word, "Obloquy", that suggests the idea of public disgrace, which in this poem is really the private disgrace of the initial rejection suffered by the lover. "The 'uncomforted actor' is presented as a lime-lit Romeo figure in the opening stanza climbing the famous balcony. Expressing love, however, can be quite uncomfortable and leads to the idea that the 'persona' who 'chirps' is both themselves and stranger at the same time. Still, the act of loving is an expansion, a flight of the heart, in which anyone can recognize and greet the other in the person who loves. Ironically the object of love disappears at this point."

[60] Elizabeth (Libby) Wong writes, "The world's antipathy towards refugees and new immigrants makes us see a lot of hate, anger, frustration and cruelty. Belief in humanity, however, tells us that, while all this is going on, there are wide-eyed innocents who believe that there is kindness and goodness

in the world. They believe there are people in the world who stretch out a helping hand towards refugees or new immigrants with understanding and compassion. The poem, 'She Believes', describes that innocence and belief in the goodness of mankind. She believes wrongly. Still she believes."

[61] Cindy Wyles explains the origins of her poem, 'Vanity Fair'. as follows: "I was exercising on an Ergo (rowing machine) when I saw my twin. I no longer felt special; there was someone who at least physically could have been a duplicate of myself. I didn't know about the recent successful UK ITV serialisation of *Vanity Fair*, when I wrote this poem—but I knew the book as part of an MA that I had taken in Victorian Literature. I liked the idea of a carousel or merry-go-round and so I tried to put the idea of this circular, no-escape motion into my poem. I connected this to the idea of time, the fingers moving on a clock or the pages being torn off a calendar. Michael Palin's introduction to the TV series uses the same device—maybe a co-incidence, or maybe evocative writing by Thackeray. I also wanted to convey the heavy feeling of moral/religious censure, which is often directed at things like vanity, which are, after all, only part of our general human frailty. Hence my reference to Mary Shelley's *Frankenstein*, another Victorian work."

[62] Anthea Yip's, 'Dragon's breath/Inspiration', is, "like a paradox, like a writer writing about writing, or a thinker thinking about thinking. This poem describes how inspiration is born, how the thought blooms in our head and how we foster it until it is ready to be placed onto paper. The process is jittery, messy, and comes in spurts of energy, just like the fragmented rhythm of the poem. The auditory aspect of the poem coincides with the sounds of a machine, which in this case, is a metaphor for our brain. The process of inspiration is timeless and untouchable, and always a product of our ever-changing identity. The end of my poem emphasises this: how each creation of ours holds our fingerprint."

ADVANCE RESPONSES

What a pleasure to browse the "mingled voices" of the third Proverse anthology—a rich and varied collection indeed: universal experiences of belonging and alienation, love and loss, sorrow and joy, expressed through vivid images, personal stories and creative patterns of language. Take your time, dear reader, dip in and out, find your own favourites and be inspired to take up your pen or switch on your laptop and write.

—**Pauline Burton, poet and educator, UK and HK**

'The Fog' in *Mingled Voices 3* begins with a line from Francis Thompson, "All's vast that vastness means."
For me, this opening of the Sanja Särman poem captures the diversity and expansiveness of each piece within the anthology. Reviewing the works has been an unexpected journey granting respect and an immensity to the condition of advanced dementia as well as to the experience of a prayerful hospice worker. It is well worth the read.

—**Dr Charles Lowe,**
Associate Dean, Division of Humanities and Social Sciences, United International College.

SOME POETRY AND POETRY COLLECTIONS
Published by Proverse Hong Kong

Alphabet, by Andrew S. Guthrie. 2015.

Astra and Sebastian, by L.W. Illsley. 2011.

Bliss of Bewilderment, by Birgit Bunzel Linder. 2017.

The Burning Lake, by Jonathan Locke Hart. 2016.

Celestial Promise, by Hayley Ann Solomon. 2017.

Chasing light, by Patricia Glinton Meicholas. 2013.

China suite and other poems,
by Gillian Bickley. 2009.

For the record and other poems of Hong Kong,
by Gillian Bickley. 2003.

Frida Kahlo's cry and other poems,
by Laura Solomon. 2015.

Heart to Heart: Poems, by Patty Ho. 2010.

Home, away, elsewhere,
by Vaughan Rapatahana. 2011.

Immortelle and bhandaaraa poems,
by Lelawattee Manoo-Rahming. 2011.

In vitro, by Laura Solomon. 2nd ed. 2014.

Irreverent poems for pretentious people,
by Henrik Hoeg. 2016.

The layers between (essays and poems),
by Celia Claase. 2015.

Of leaves & ashes, by Patty Ho. 2016.

Life Lines, by Shahilla Shariff. 2011.

Mingled voices: the international Proverse Poetry Prize anthology 2016,
edited by Gillian and Verner Bickley. 2017.

Mingled voices 2: the international Proverse Poetry Prize anthology 2017,
edited by Gillian and Verner Bickley. 2018.

Moving house and other poems from Hong Kong,
by Gillian Bickley. 2005.

Over the Years: Selected Collected Poems, 1972-2015,
by Gillian Bickley. 2017.

Painting the borrowed house: poems,
by Kate Rogers. 2008.

Perceptions, by Gillian Bickley. 2012.

Rain on the pacific coast,
by Elbert Siu Ping Lee. 2013.

refrain, by Jason S. Polley. 2010.

Shadow play, by James Norcliffe. 2012.

Shadows in deferment, by Birgit Bunzel Linder. 2013.

Shifting sands, by Deepa Vanjani. 2016.

Sightings: a collection of poetry, with an essay, 'communicating poems', by Gillian Bickley. 2007.

Smoked pearl: poems of Hong Kong and beyond,
by Akin Jeje (Akinsola Olufemi Jeje). 2010.

Of symbols misused, by Mary-Jane Newton. 2011.

Unlocking, by Mary-Jane Newton. March 2014.

Violet, by Carolina Ilica. March 2019.

Wonder, lust & itchy feet, by Sally Dellow. 2011.

FIND OUT MORE ABOUT OUR AUTHORS, BOOKS, EVENTS AND LITERARY PRIZES

Visit our website: http://www.proversepublishing.com

Visit our distributor's website: www.chineseupress.com

Follow us on Twitter
Follow news and conversation: twitter.com/Proversebooks
OR
Copy and paste the following to your browser window and follow the instructions:
https://twitter.com/#!/ProverseBooks

"Like" us on www.facebook.com/ProversePress

Request our free E-Newsletter
Send your request to info@proversepublishing.com.

Availability
Available in Hong Kong and world-wide from our Hong Kong based distributor, The Chinese University of Hong Kong Press, The Chinese University of Hong Kong, Shatin, NT, Hong Kong SAR, China.
Email: cup-bus@cuhk.edu.hk
Website: www.chineseupress.com.
All titles are available from Proverse Hong Kong, http://www.proversepublishing.com

Stock-holding retailers
Hong Kong (CUHKP, Bookazine)
Canada (Elizabeth Campbell Books),
Andorra (Llibreria La Puça, La Llibreria).

Orders may be made from bookshops in the UK and elsewhere.

Ebooks
Most of our titles are available also as Ebooks.

Made in the USA
Middletown, DE
19 March 2020